CELTIC THUNDER
MYTHOLOGY

ISBN 978-1-4803-6266-6

HAL•LEONARD®
CORPORATION

7777 W. BLUEMOUND RD. P.O. BOX 13819 MILWAUKEE, WI 53213

Visit Hal Leonard Online at
www.halleonard.com

4 VOICES

16 THE ISLE OF INNISFREE

21 NOW WE ARE FREE

28 SCARLET RIBBONS (FOR HER HAIR)

35 THE ROCKY ROAD TO DUBLIN

43 CARRICKFERGUS

49 HOEDOWN

57 DANNY BOY

62 HUNTER'S MOON

71 SHE MOVED THROUGH THE FAIR

77 CAROLINA RUA

83 TURNING AWAY

91 TEARS OF HERCULES

96 MY LAND

* Due to licensing restrictions,
  "Katie" is not included in this folio.

VOICES

By DAVID MUNRO
and BRENDAN GRAHAM

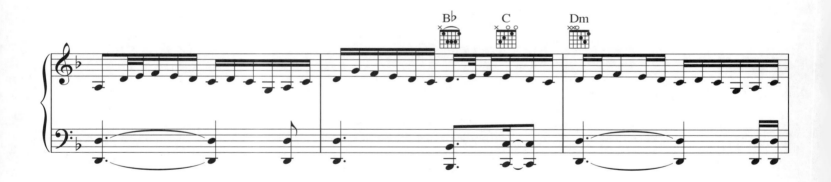

5

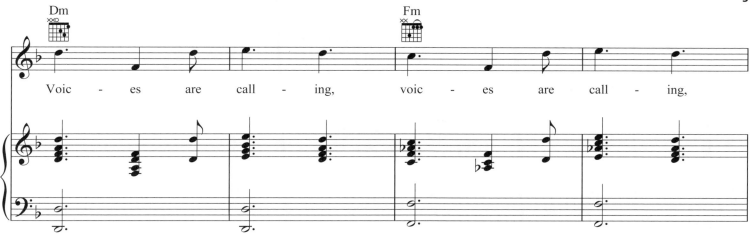

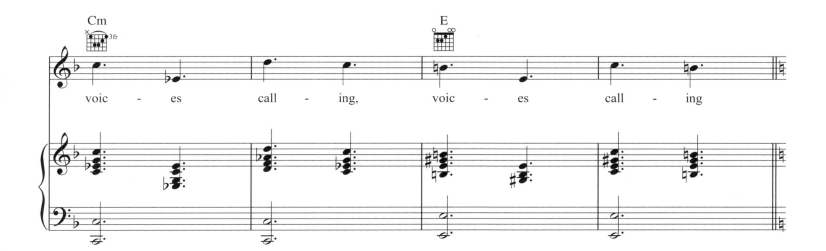

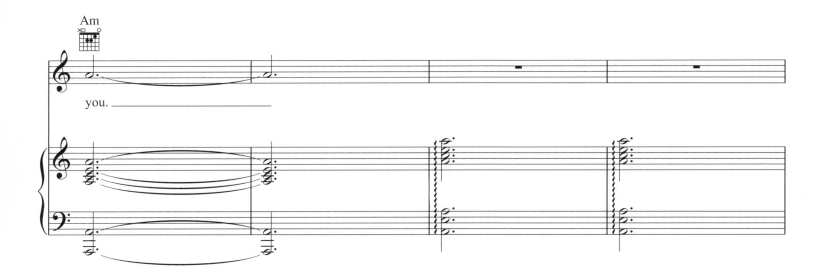

With a lilt

There's a voice ___ that is start-ing to call ___ us. There's a voice ___ that we

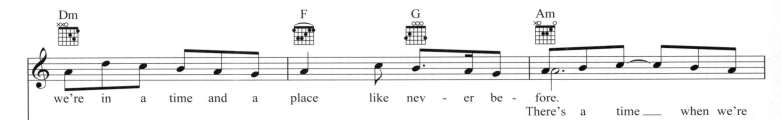

just can't ig - nore. There's a bell ___ that is ring-ing to tell ___ us,

we're in a time and a place like nev - er be - fore. There's a time ___ when we're

called to be read - y. It's a time ___ when a sign will ap - pear.

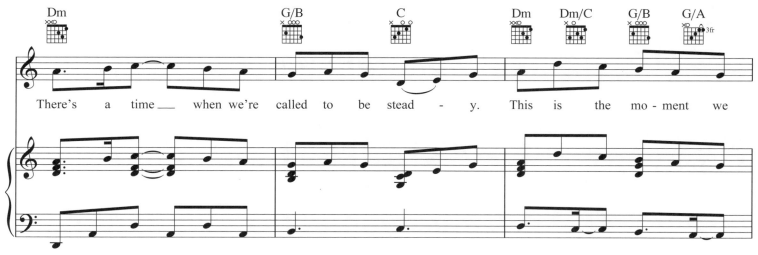

There's a time ___ when we're called to be stead - y. This is the mo - ment we

know, that the mo - ment is here.

Why is it we are here? ___ Where is it we will go? ___

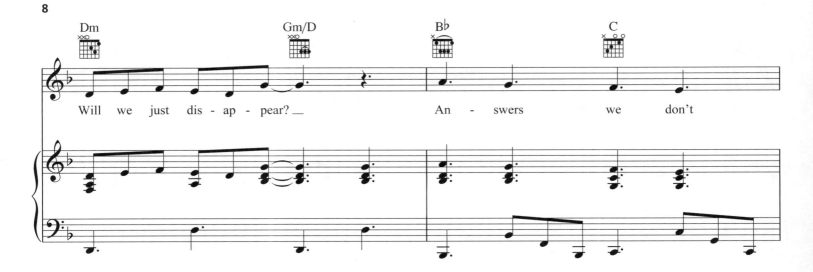

Will we just dis - ap - pear? __ An - swers we don't

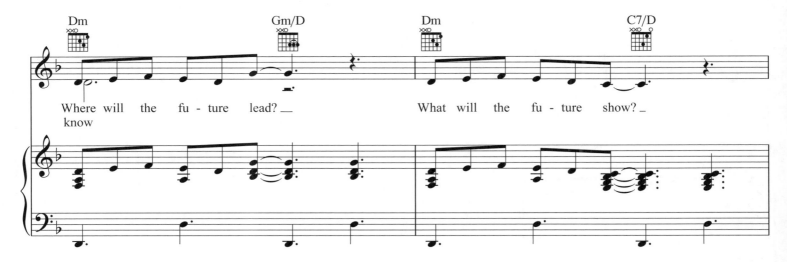

Where will the fu - ture lead? __ What will the fu - ture show? __
know

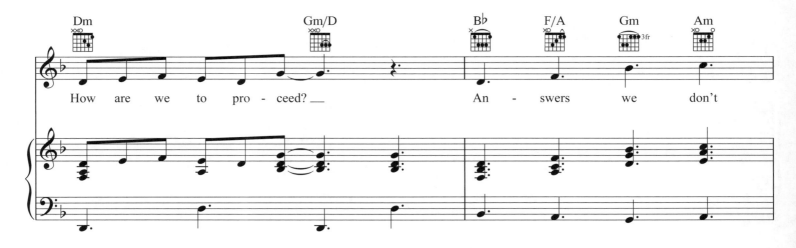

How are we to pro - ceed? __ An - swers we don't

know.

Why is it we are here? Where is it we will

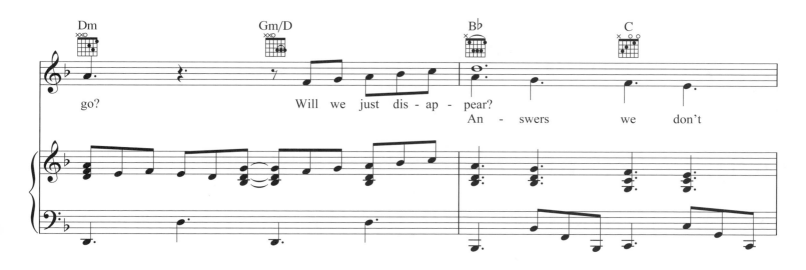

go? Will we just dis-ap-pear? An-swers we don't

know. Where will the fu-ture lead? What will our fu-ture

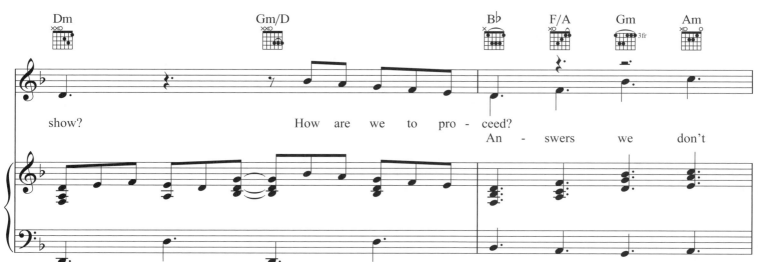

show? How are we to pro-ceed? An-swers we don't

10

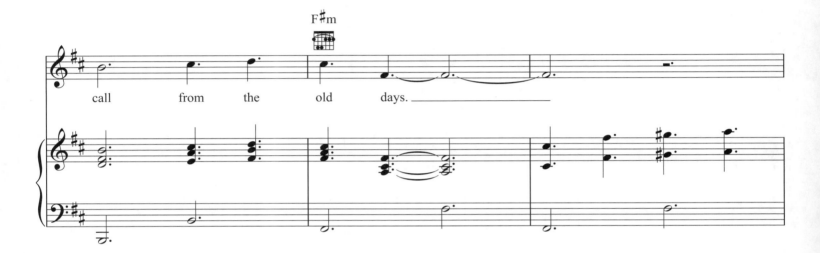

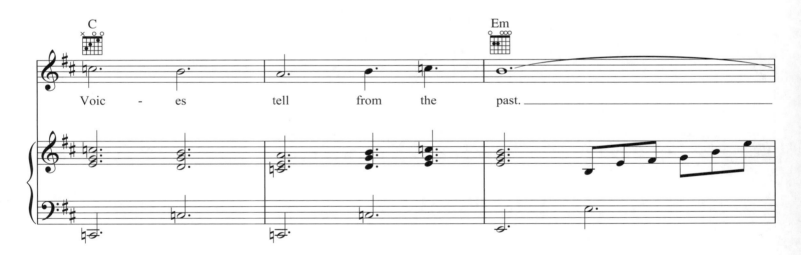

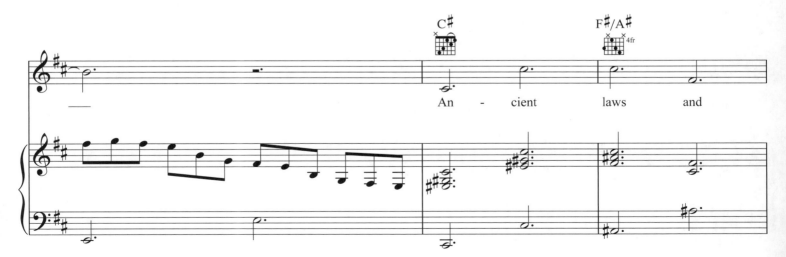

an - cient old ways to _____ re - cast. _____

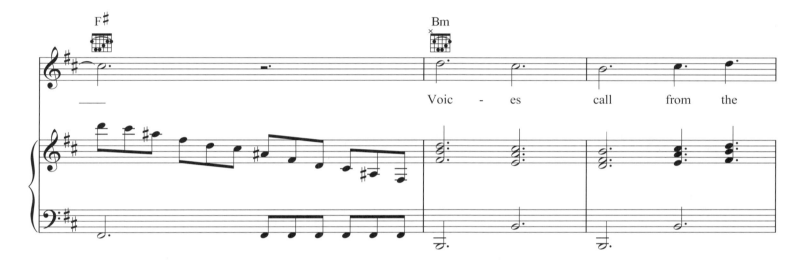

_____ Voic - es call from the

fu - ture. _____ How will

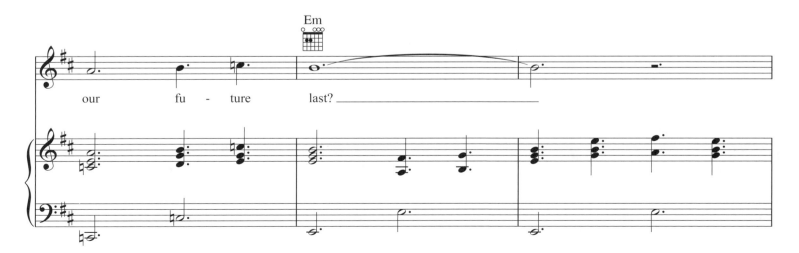

our fu - ture last? _____

THE ISLE OF INNISFREE

Words and Music by
DICK FARRELY

Lyrics:

I've met some folks who say that I'm a dream-er. And I've no doubt there's truth in what they say. But sure a bod-y is bound to be a dream-er when all the things he loves are far a-way. And pre-cious

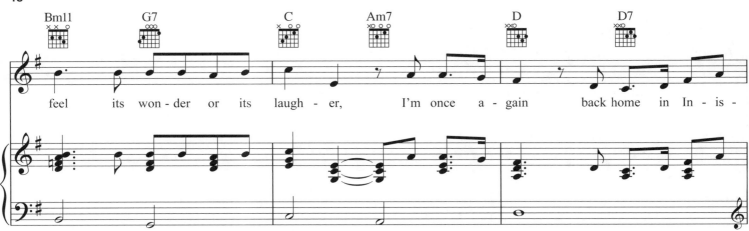

feel its won-der or its laugh-er, I'm once a-gain back home in In-is-

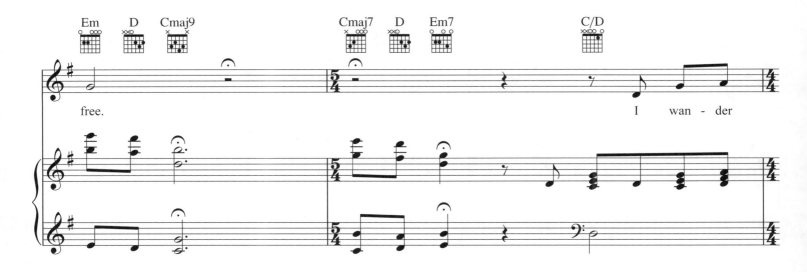

free. I wan-der

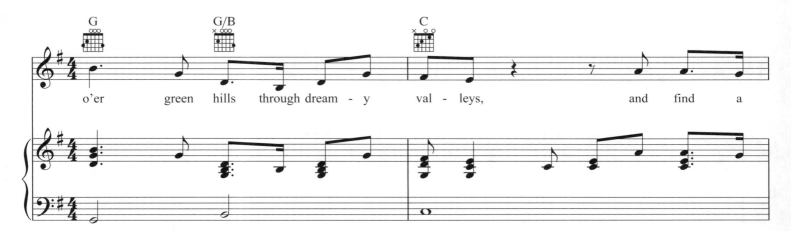

o'er green hills through dream-y val-leys, and find a

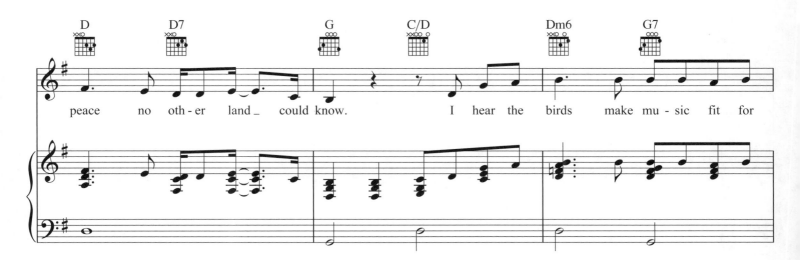

peace no oth-er land _ could know. I hear the birds make mu-sic fit for

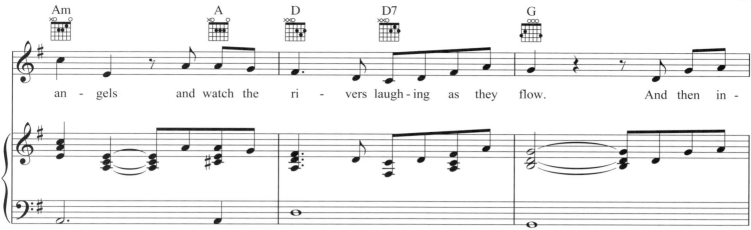

an - gels and watch the ri - vers laugh - ing as they flow. And then in -

to a hum - ble shack I wan - der, my dear old home and ten - der - ly be -

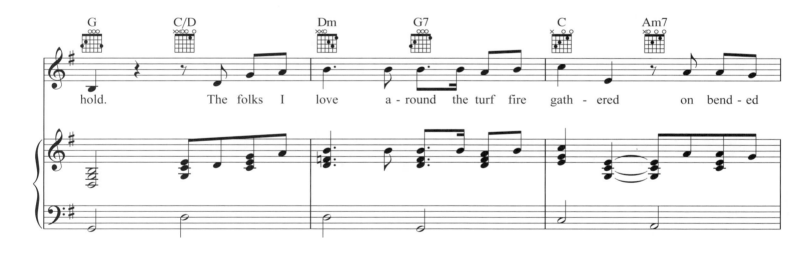

hold. The folks I love a - round the turf fire gath - ered on bend - ed

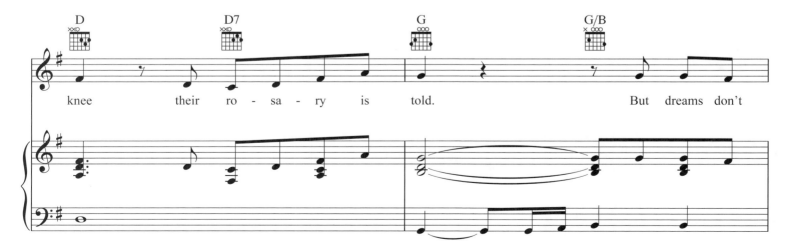

knee their ro - sa - ry is told. But dreams don't

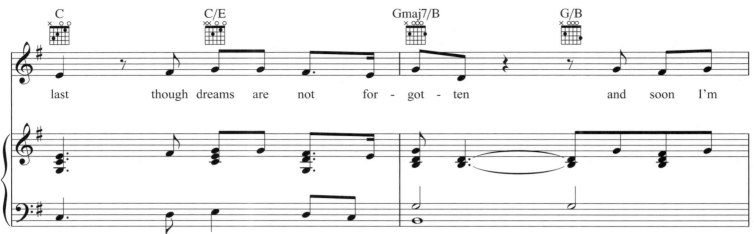

last though dreams are not for - got - ten and soon I'm

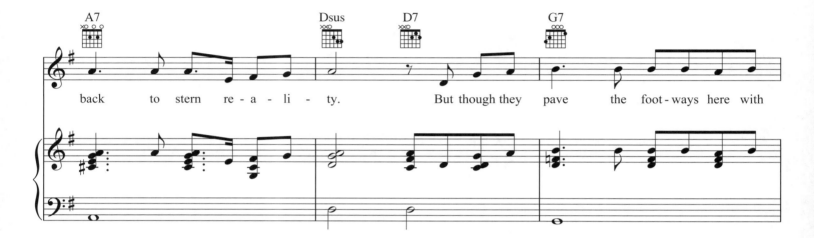

back to stern re - a - li - ty. But though they pave the foot - ways here with

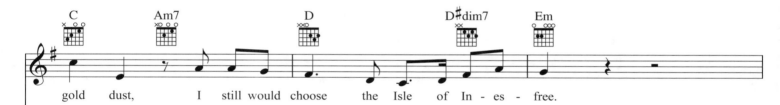

gold dust, I still would choose the Isle of In - es - free.

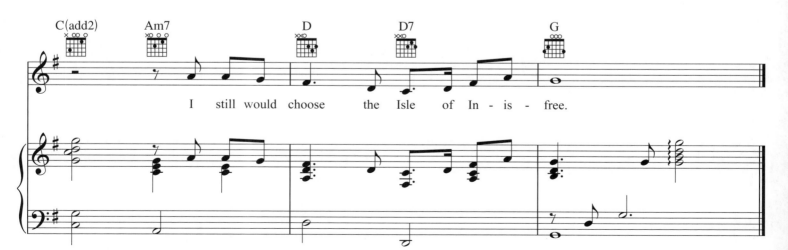

I still would choose the Isle of In - is - free.

NOW WE ARE FREE

from the DreamWorks film GLADIATOR

Written by HANS ZIMMER,
LISA GERRARD and KLAUS BADELT

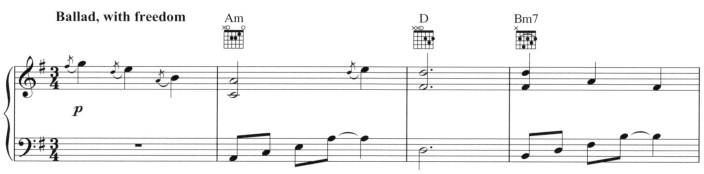

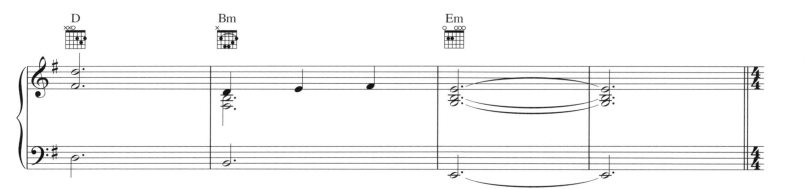

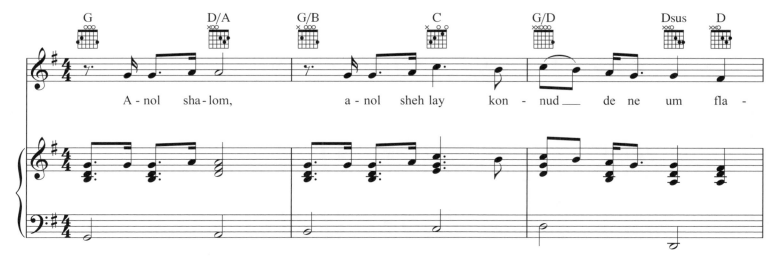

A - nol sha - lom, a - nol sheh lay kon - nud ___ de ne um fla -

22

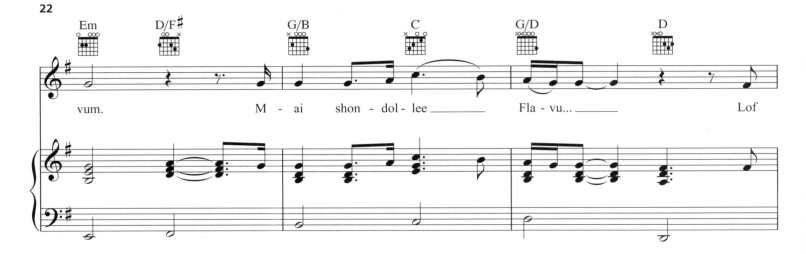

vum. M - ai shon - dol - lee _____ Fla - vu... _____ Lof

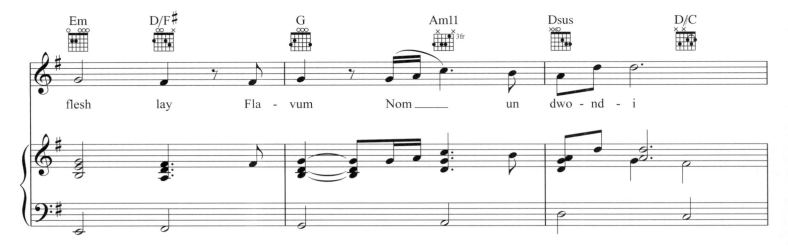

flesh lay Fla - vum Nom _____ un dwo - nd - i

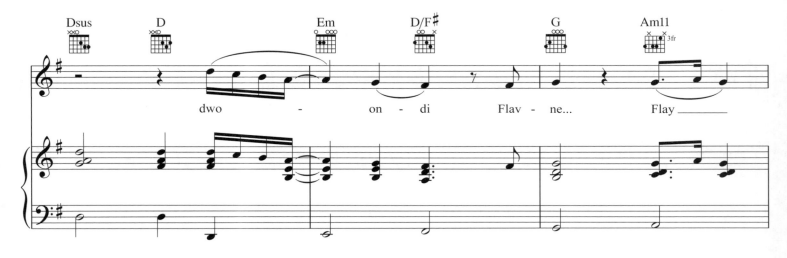

dwo - on - di Flav - ne... Flay _____

Moderate Ballad, stricter time

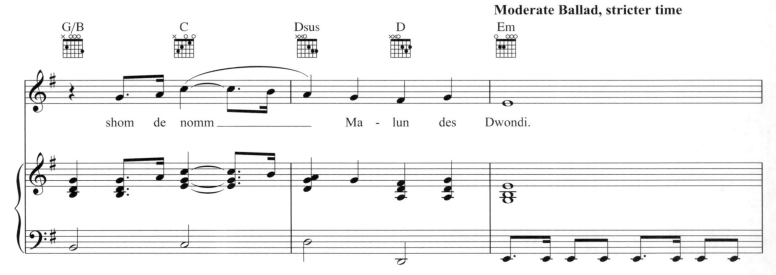

shom de nomm _____ Ma - lun des Dwondi.

23

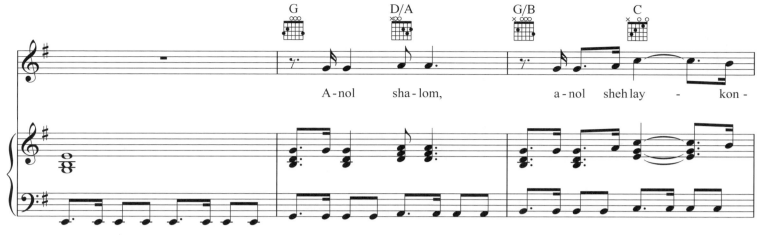

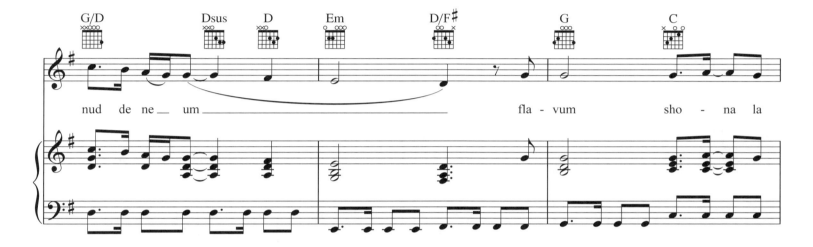

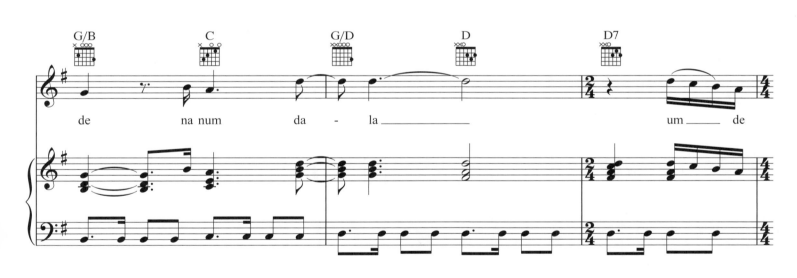

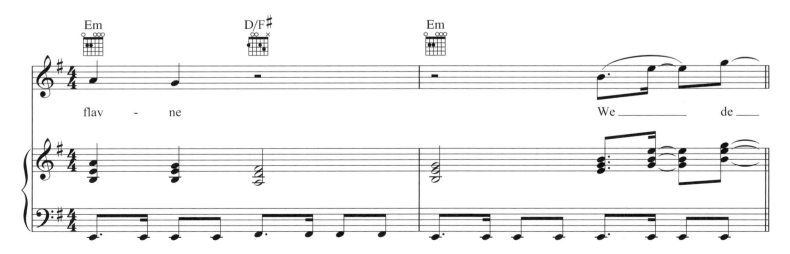

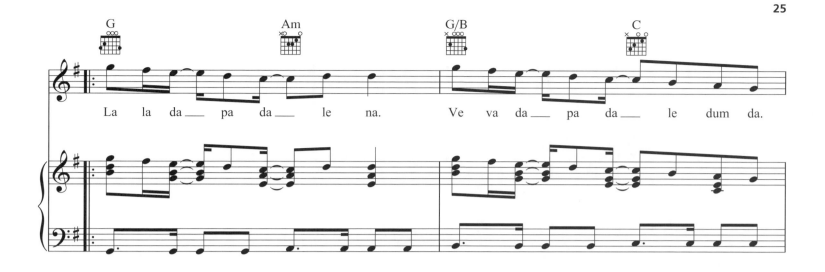

La la da __ pa da __ le na. Ve va da __ pa da __ le dum da.

La la da __ pa da __ le na. Ve va da __ pa da __ le dum da.

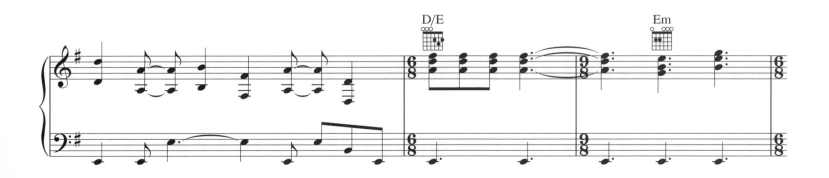

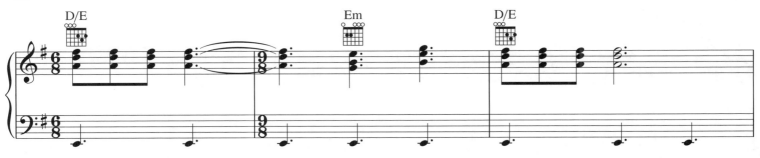

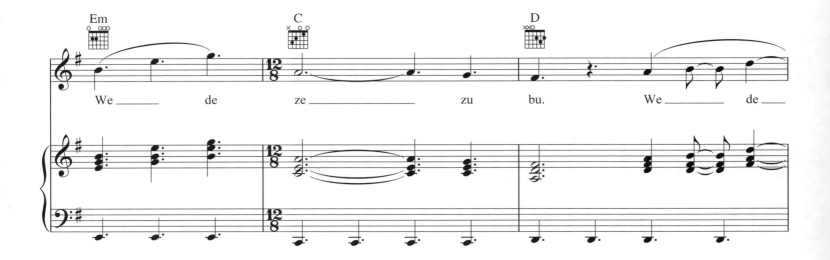

We ___ de ze ___ zu bu. We ___ de ___

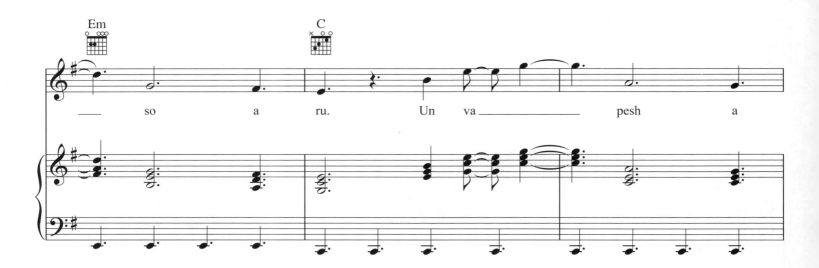

___ so a ru. Un va ___ pesh a

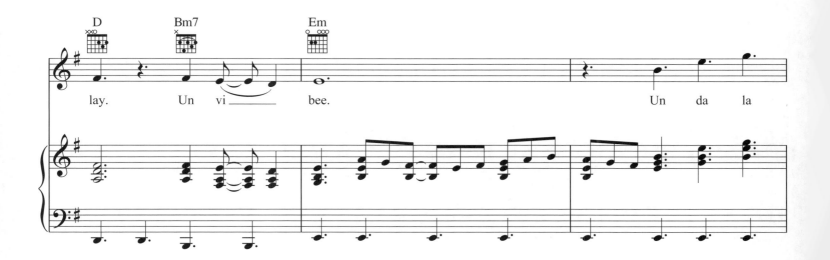

lay. Un vi ___ bee. Un da la

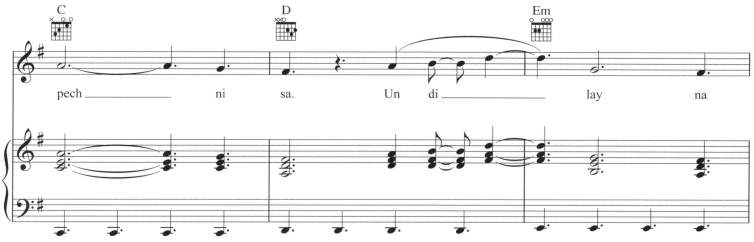

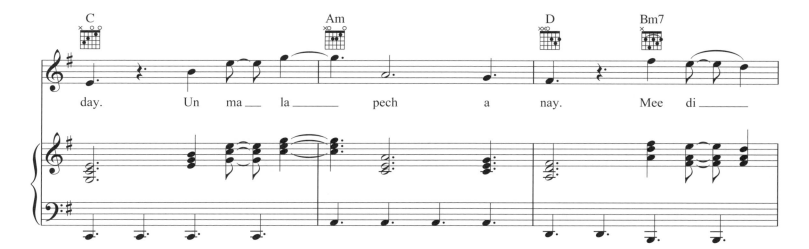

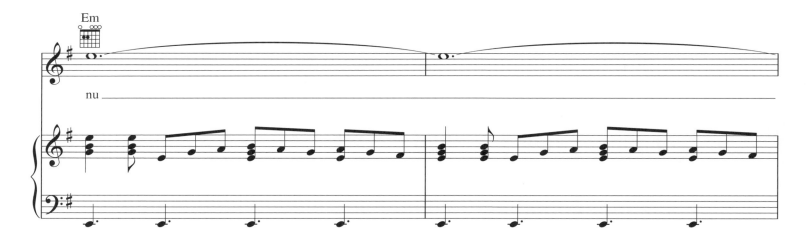

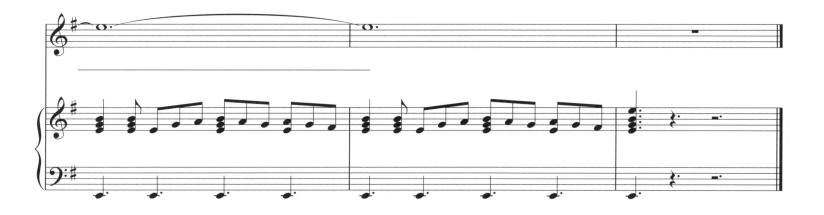

SCARLET RIBBONS
(For Her Hair)

Words by JACK SEGAL
Music by EVELYN DANZIG

Gentle Ballad

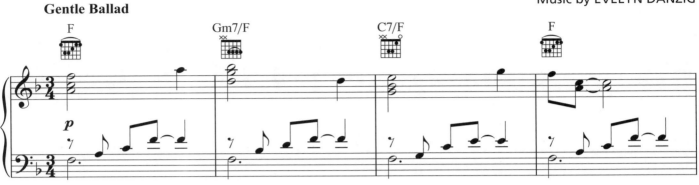

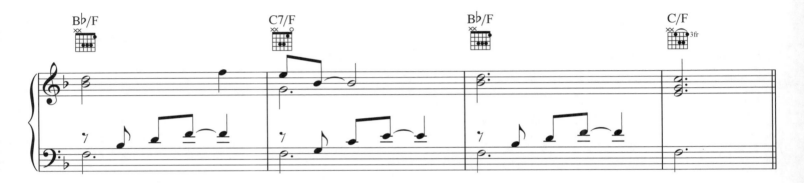

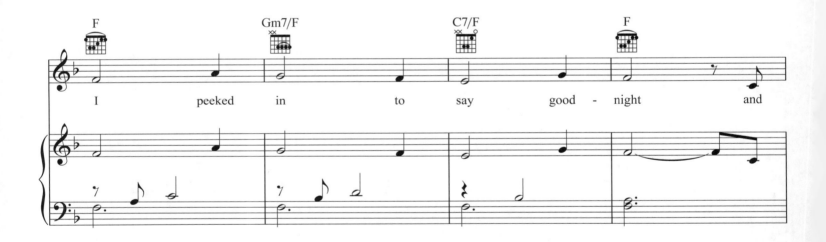

I peeked in to say good-night and

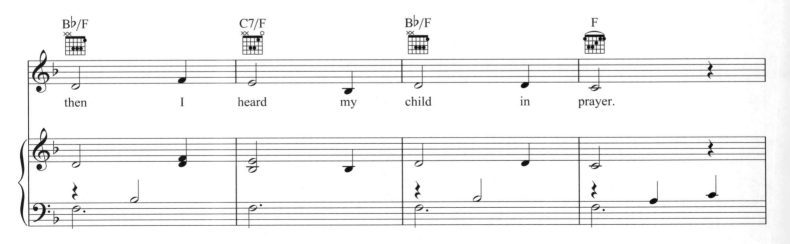

then I heard my child in prayer.

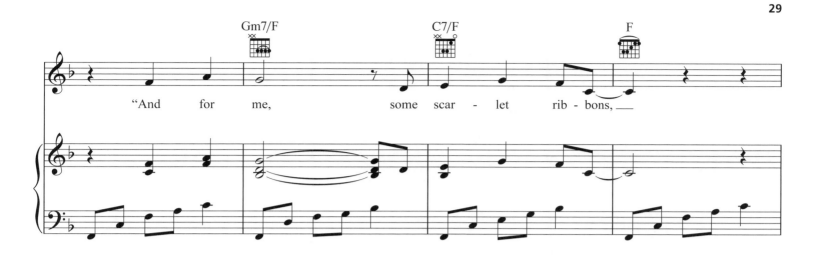

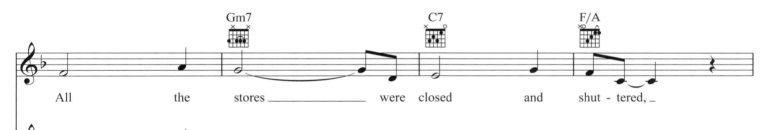

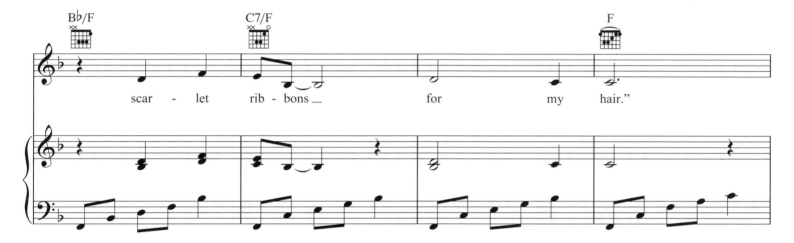

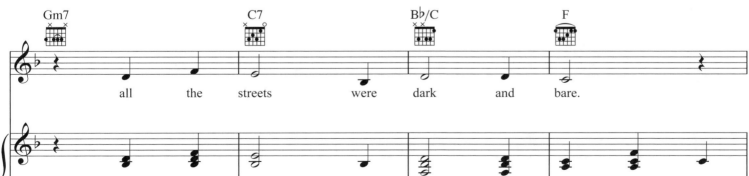

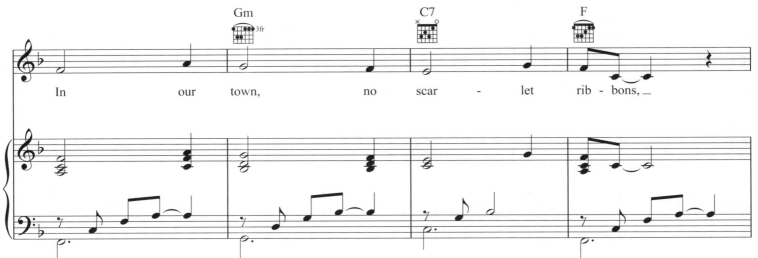

In our town, no scar - let rib - bons, __

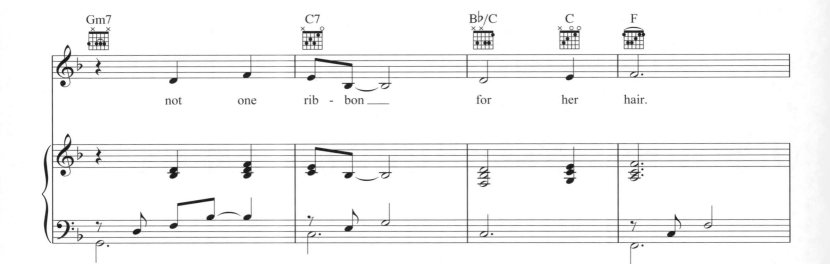

not one rib - bon __ for her hair.

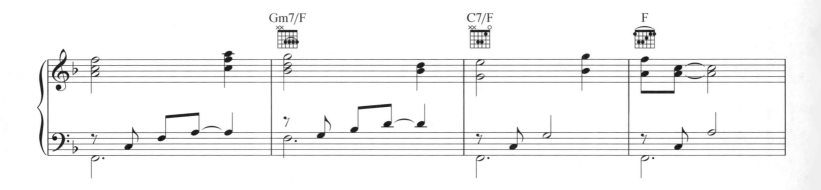

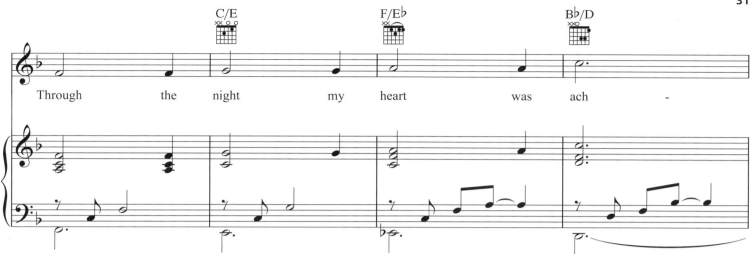

Through the night my heart was ach -

ing, just be - fore the dawn was

break - ing. I peeked in and

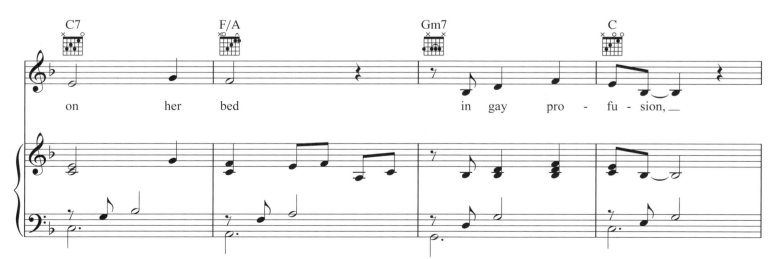

on her bed in gay pro - fu - sion, __

ly - ing there, love - ly rib - bons, __

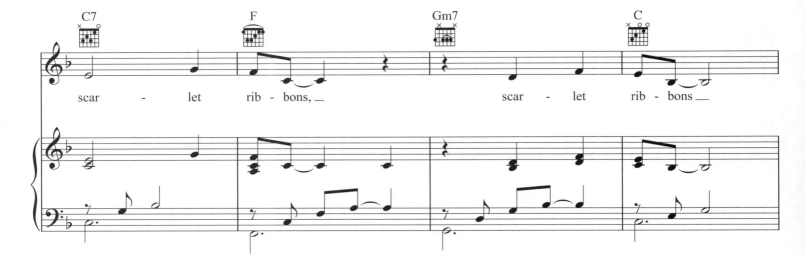

scar - let rib - bons, __ scar - let rib - bons __

for her hair.

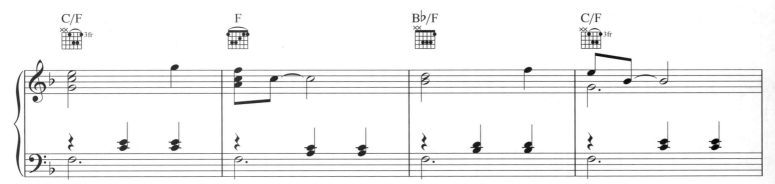

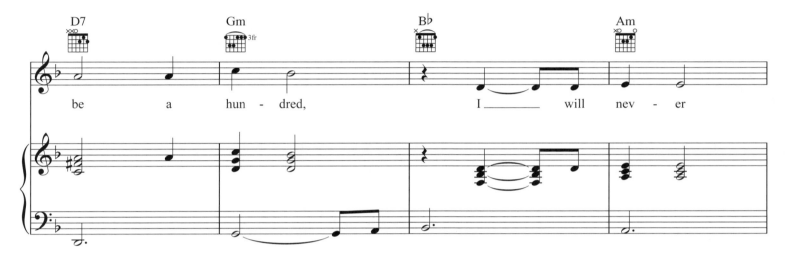

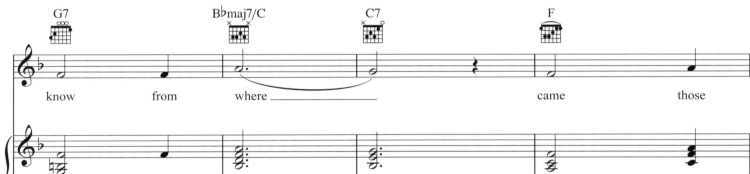

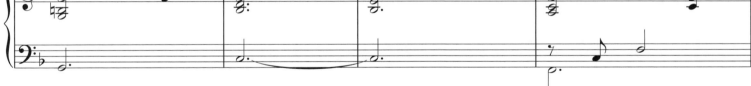

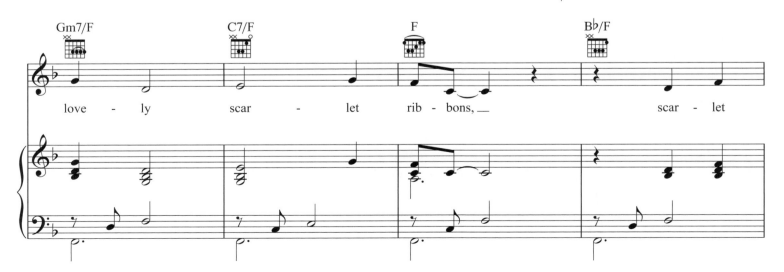

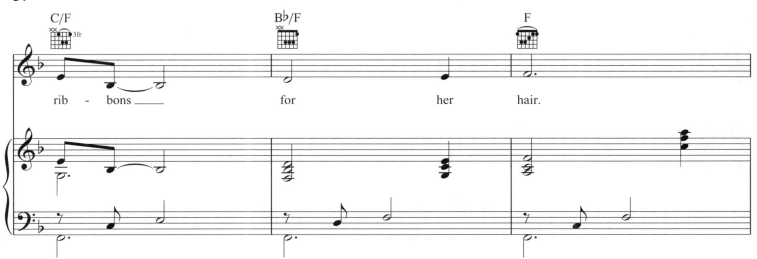

rib - bons _____ for her hair.

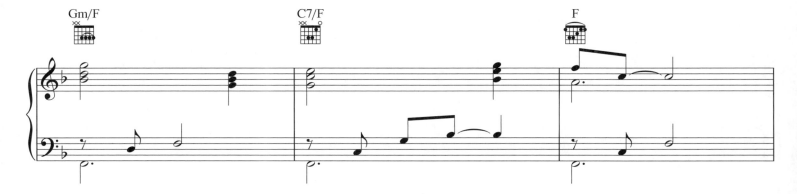

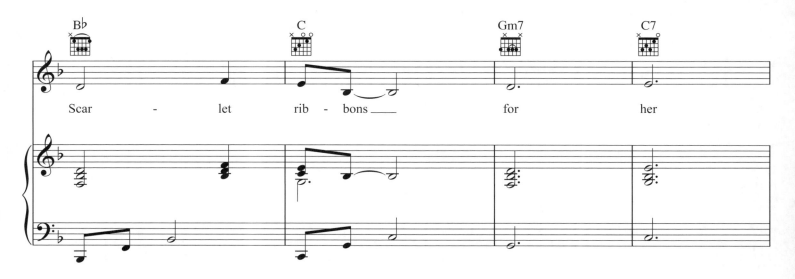

Scar - let rib - bons _____ for her

hair. _____

THE ROCKY ROAD TO DUBLIN

Arranged by
DAVID MUNRO

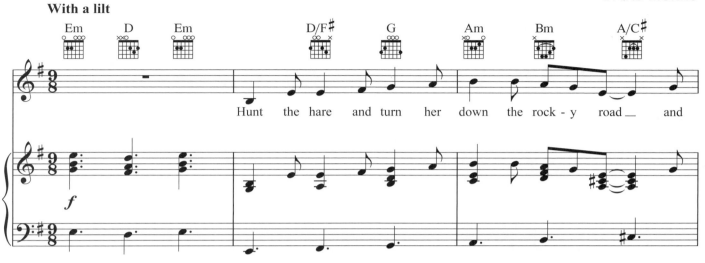

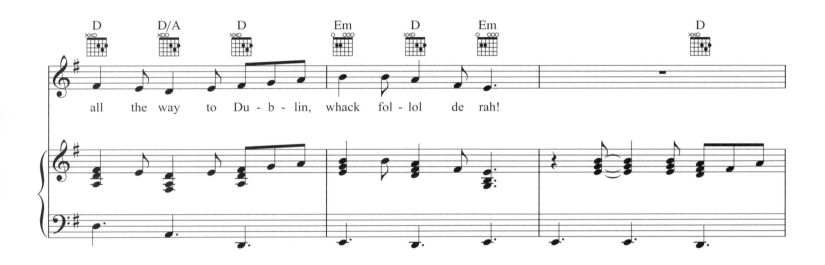

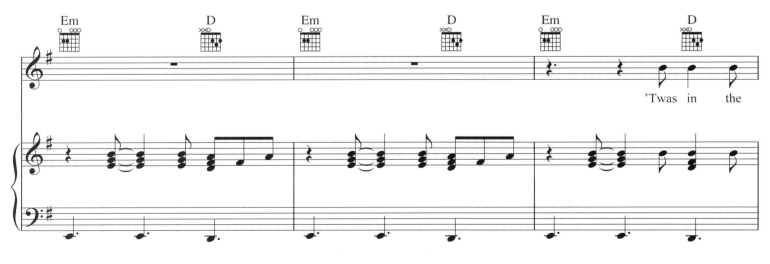

36

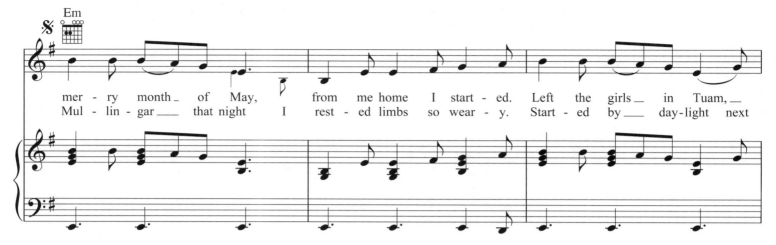

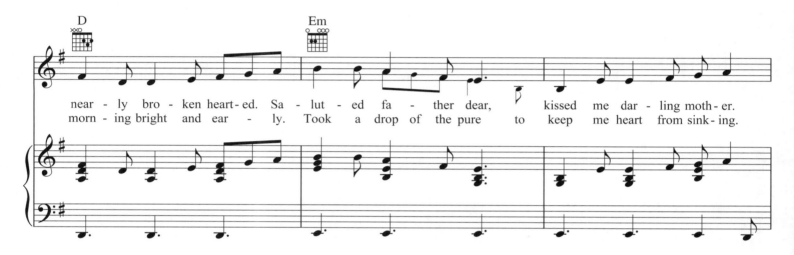

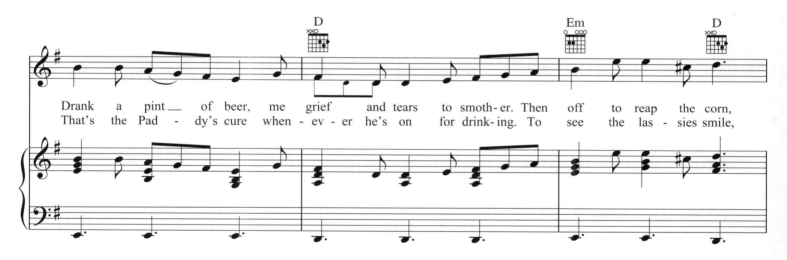

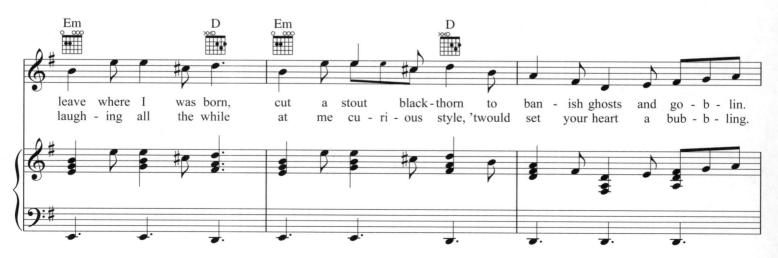

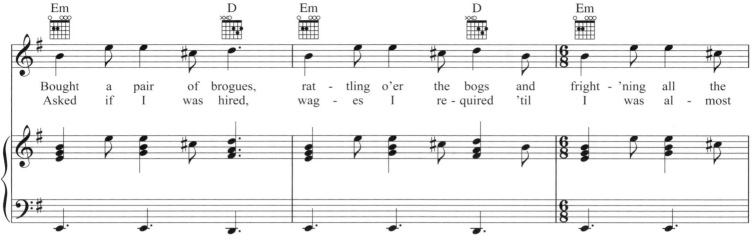

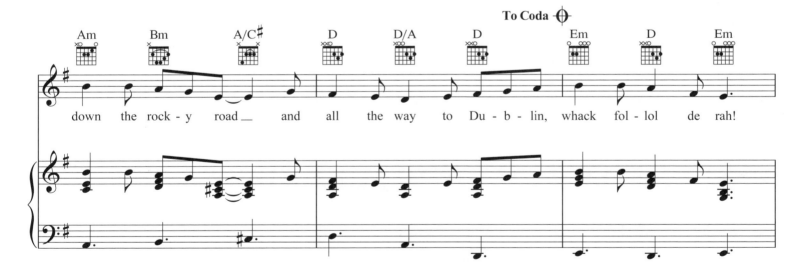

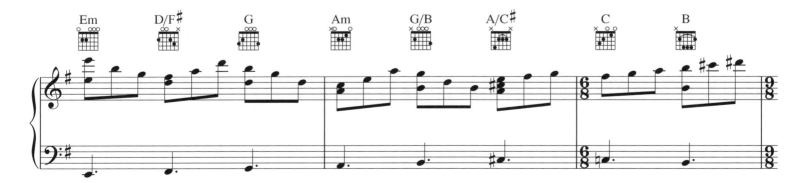

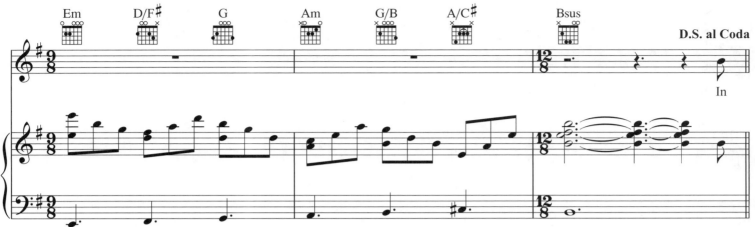

D.S. al Coda

In

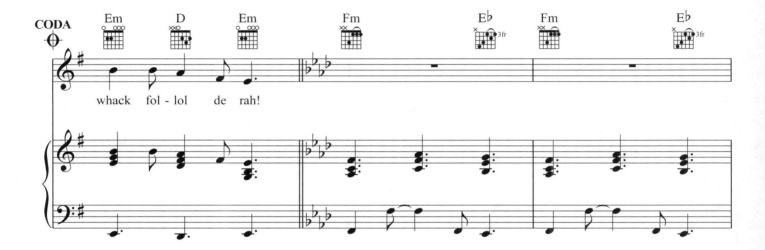

CODA

whack fol - lol de rah!

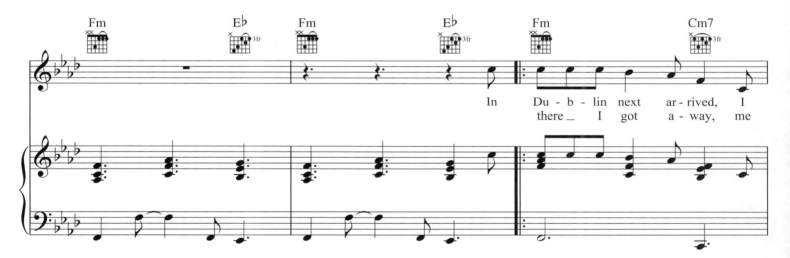

In Du - b - lin next ar - rived, I
there _ I got a - way, me

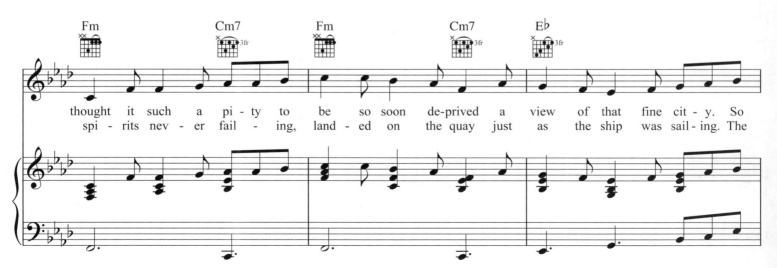

thought it such a pi - ty to be so soon de - prived a view of that fine cit - y. So
spi - rits nev - er fail - ing, land - ed on the quay just as the ship was sail - ing. The

One, two, three, four, five.
One, two, three, four, five. Hunt the hare and turn her down the rock-y road __ and

all the way to Du-b-lin, whack fol-lol de rah!

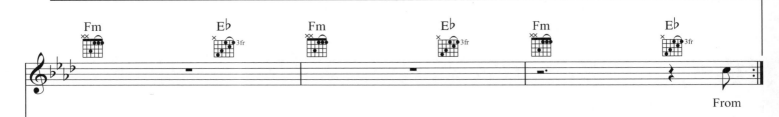

From

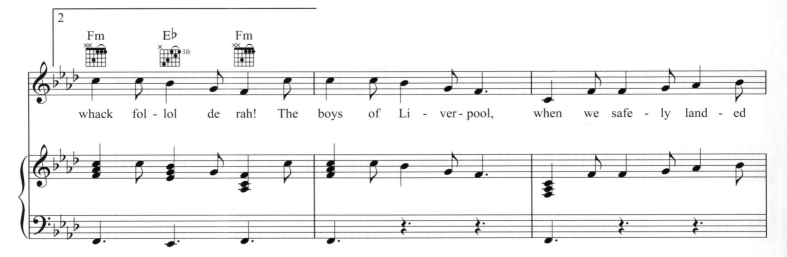

whack fol-lol de rah! The boys of Li-ver-pool, when we safe-ly land-ed

41

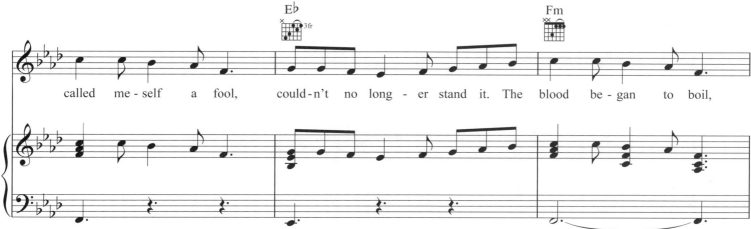

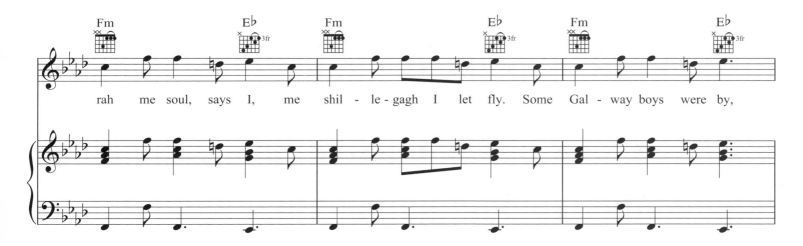

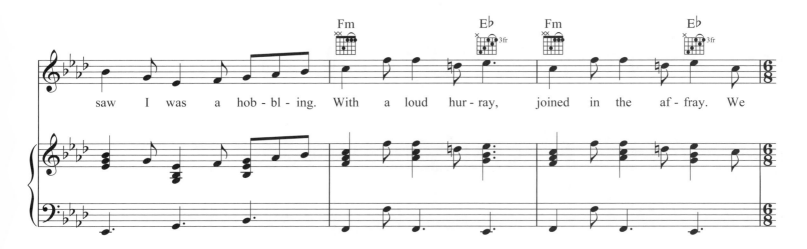

CARRICKFERGUS

Arranged by DAVID MUNRO

Gentle Ballad, with some freedom

Lyrics:
I wish I was ___ in ___ Car-rick - fer-gus. On - ly for nights ___ now, in ___ Bal - ly - gran. I would swim

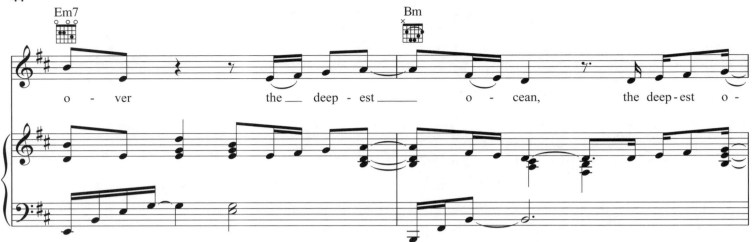

o - ver the deep-est o - cean, the deep-est o -

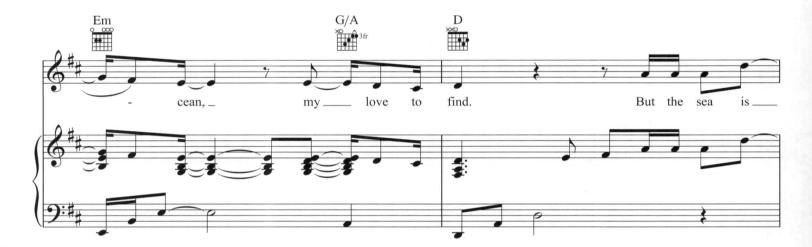

- cean, _ my _ love to find. But the sea is _

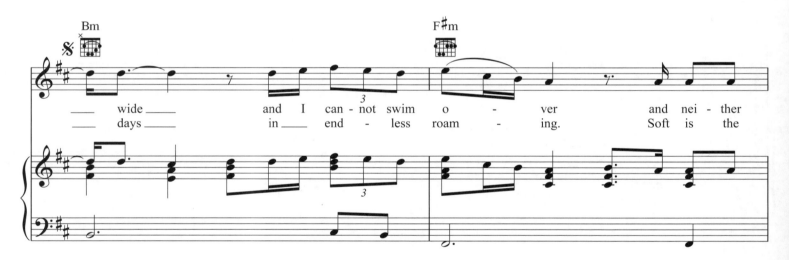

_ wide _ and I can-not swim o - ver _ and nei - ther
_ days _ in _ end-less roam - ing. Soft is the

have _ I the wings to fly. If I could
grass, _ my bed is free. Ah, to be

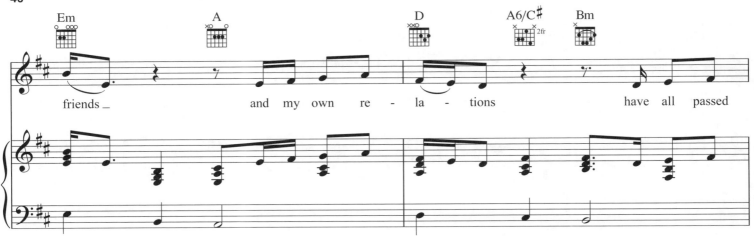

friends __ and my own re - la - tions have all passed

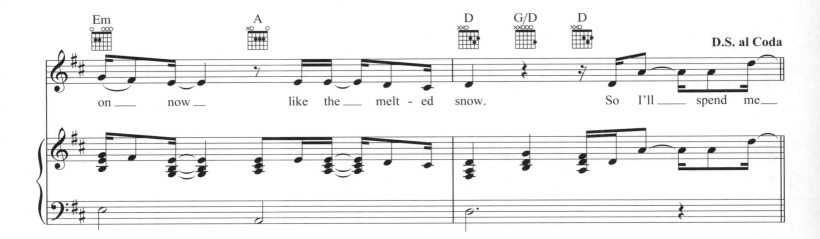

D.S. al Coda

on __ now __ like the __ melt - ed snow. So I'll __ spend me __

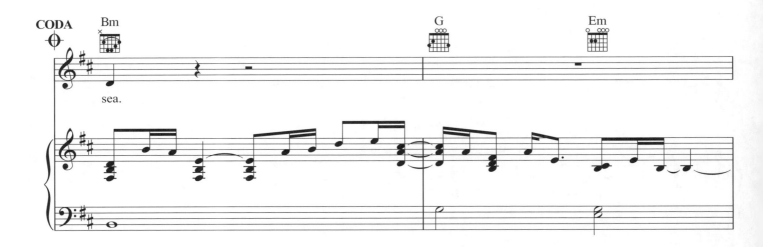

CODA

sea.

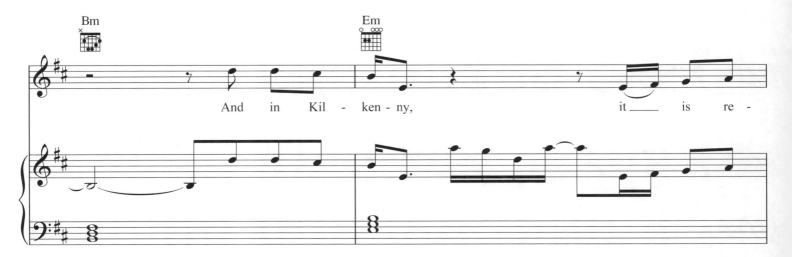

And in Kil - ken - ny, it __ is re -

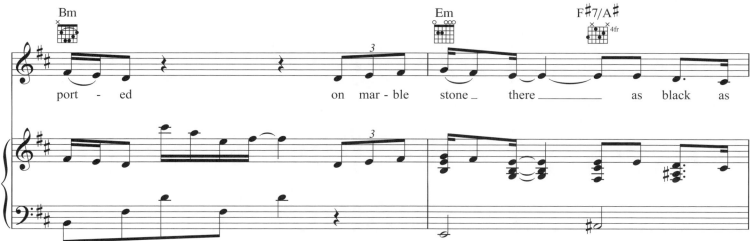

on marble stone there as black as

ink. With gold and silver, I would sup-

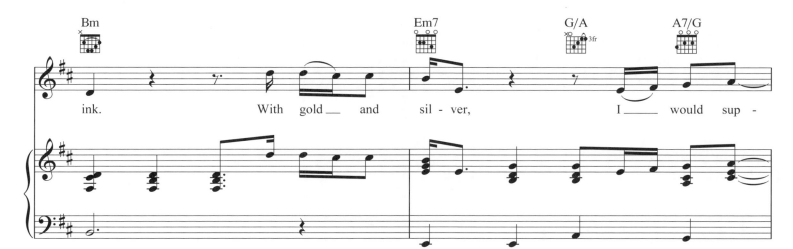

-port her. But I'll sing no more now 'til I get a

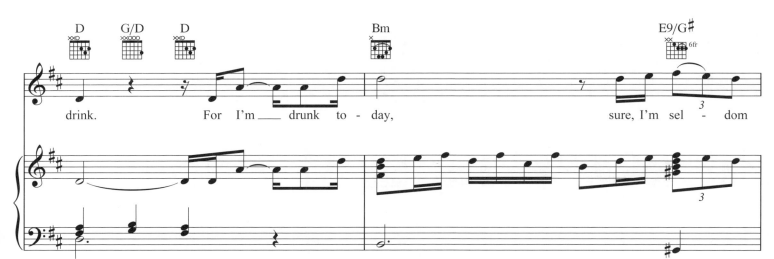

drink. For I'm drunk today, sure, I'm seldom

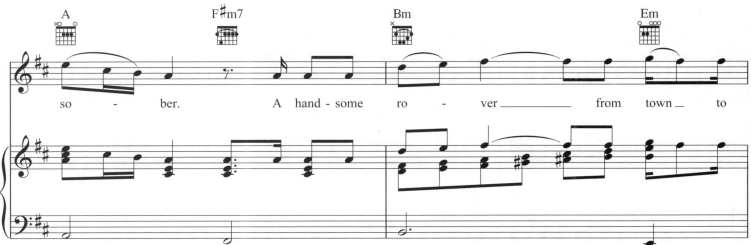

so - ber. A hand - some ro - ver _____ from town ___ to

town. _____ Ah, but I'm sick now _____ and my ___ days are ___

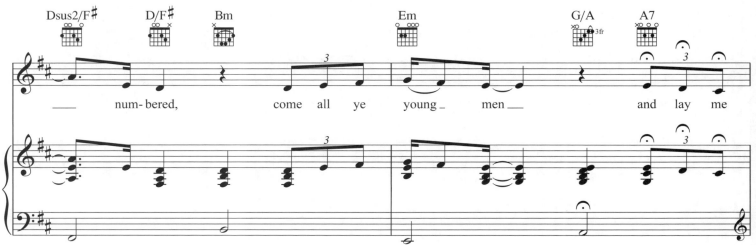

___ num- bered, come all ye young ___ men ___ and lay me

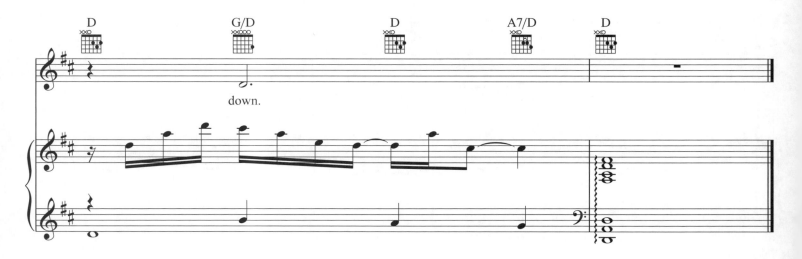

down.

HOEDOWN
from RODEO

By AARON COPLAND

With energy

54

DANNY BOY

Arranged by
DAVID MUNRO

Gentle Ballad

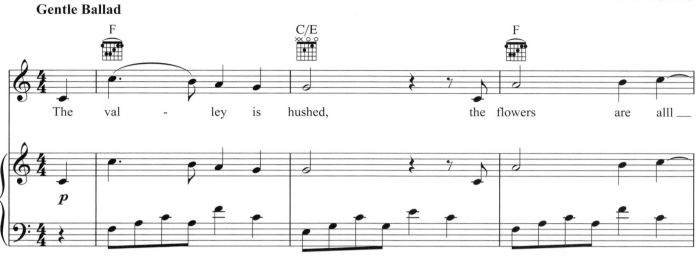

The val - ley is hushed, the flowers are alll ___

___ dy - ing. The mea - dow ___ is white

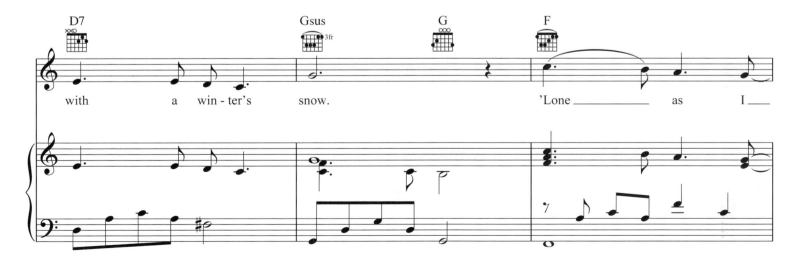

with a win - ter's snow. 'Lone ___ as I ___

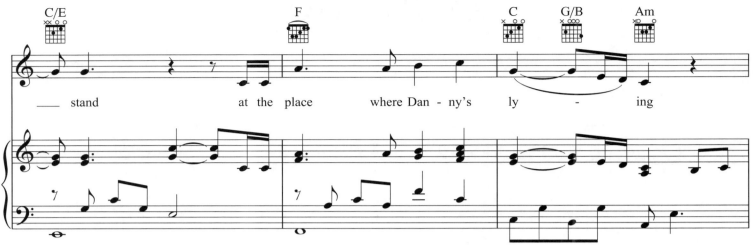

__ stand   at the place   where Dan - ny's   ly -   ing

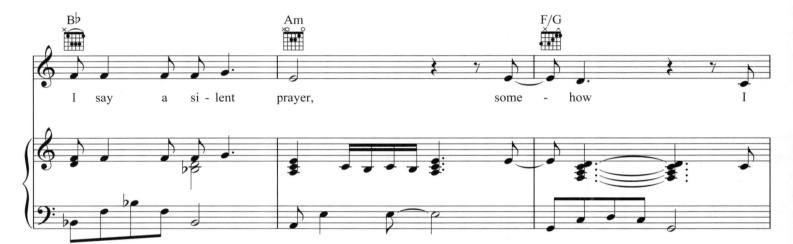

I say   a   si - lent   prayer,   some - how   I

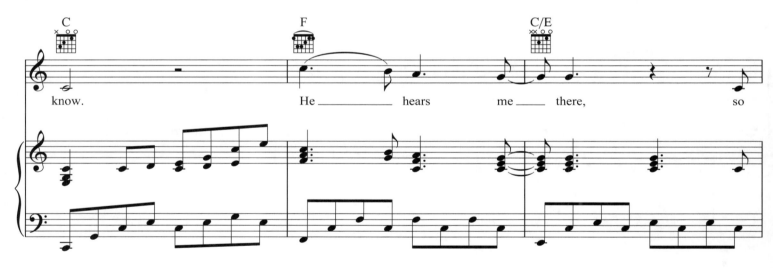

know.   He ___ hears   me __ there,   so

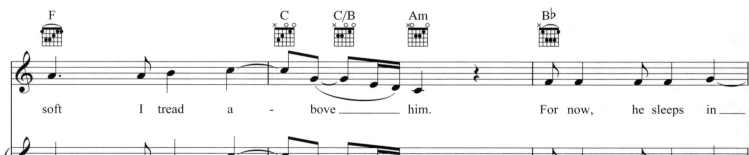

soft   I tread   a -   bove ___ him.   For now,   he sleeps in __

peace, we hear Dan-ny's voice no more.

O, Dan-ny boy, the

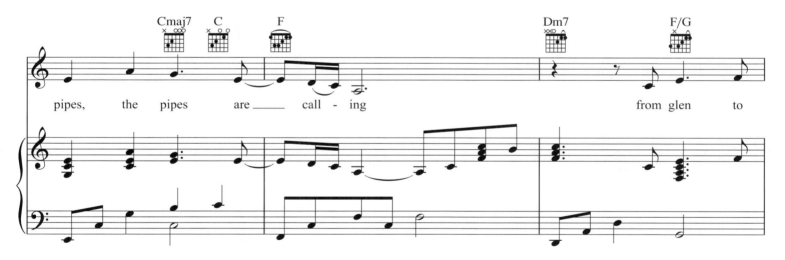

pipes, the pipes are call-ing from glen to

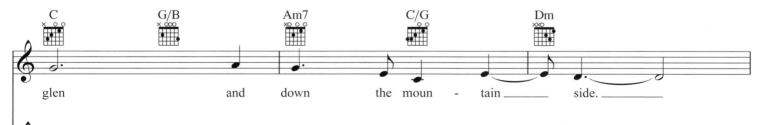

glen and down the moun-tain side.

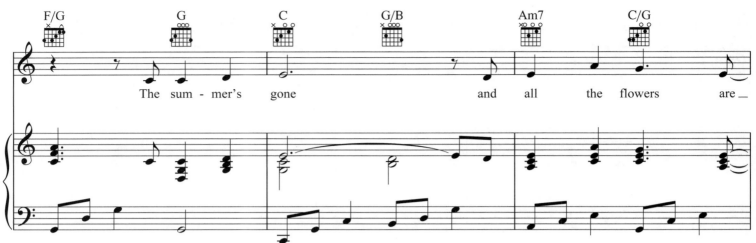

The sum - mer's gone and all the flowers are __

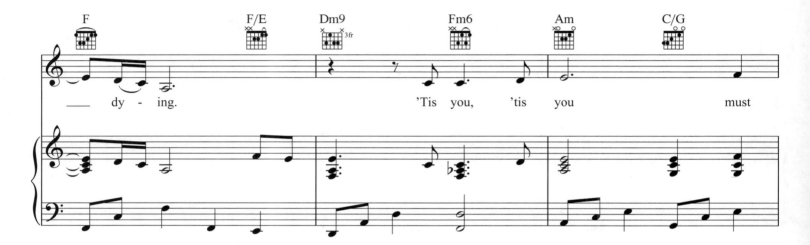

__ dy - ing. 'Tis you, 'tis you must

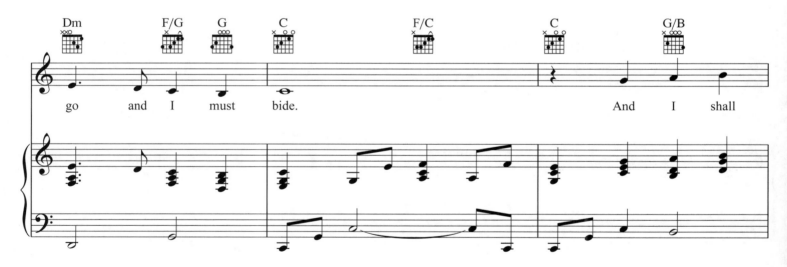

go and I must bide. And I shall

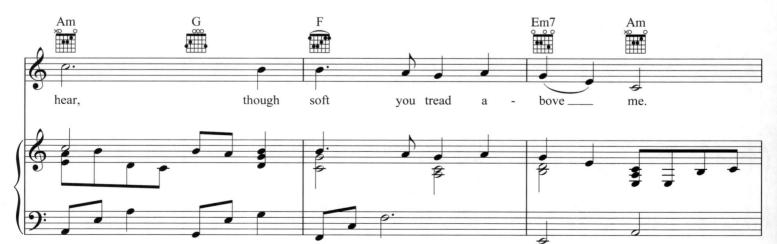

hear, though soft you tread a - bove ___ me.

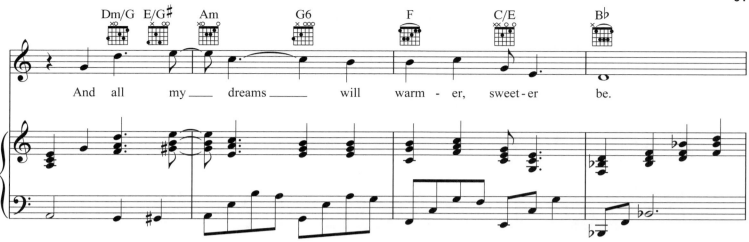

And all my ___ dreams ___ will warm - er, sweet - er be.

And you will bend and tell me that you love ___ me.

And I will sleep in peace un - til you come

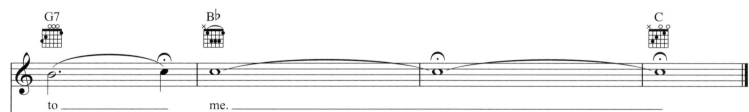

to ___ me. ___

HUNTER'S MOON

By DAVID MUNRO
and ARTHUR RIORDAN

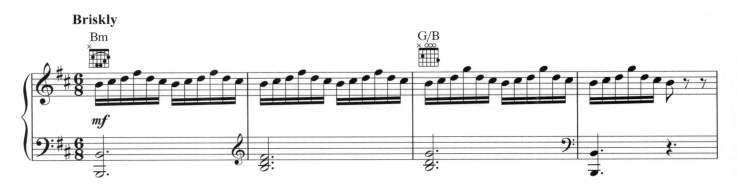

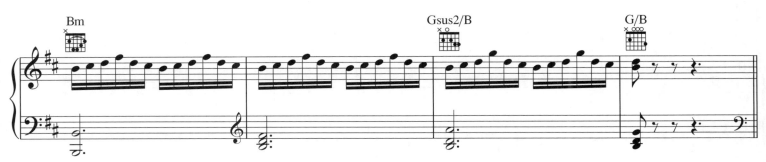

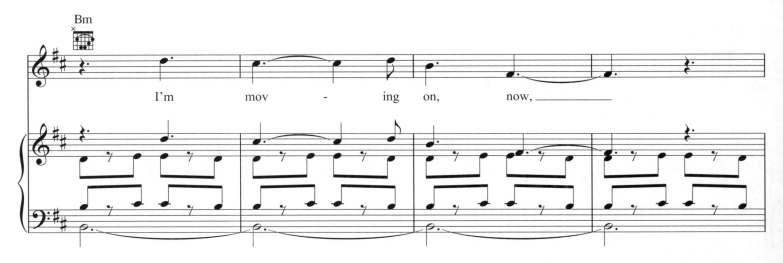

I'm mov - ing on, now, _____

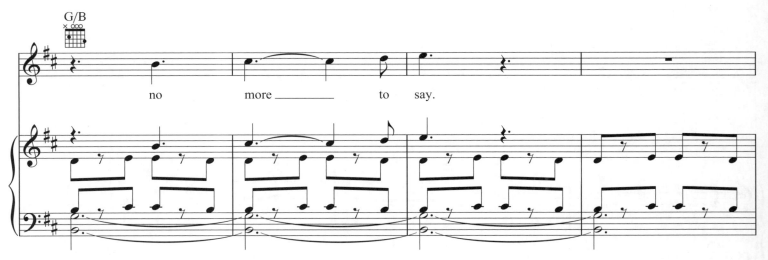

no more _____ to say.

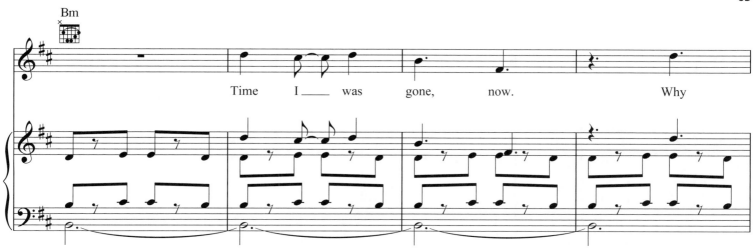

Time I ___ was gone, now.   Why

would   I   stay? _____

Don't rake ___ the ash - es,

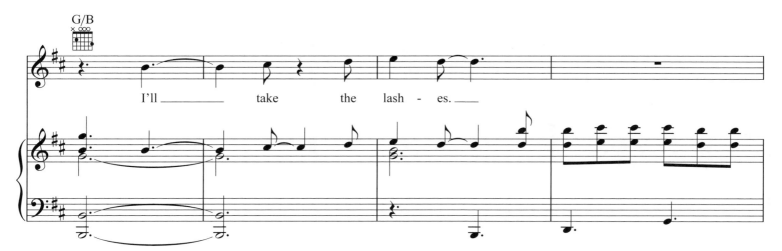

I'll _____ take the lash - es. ___

You go, now, I'll walk a -

way.

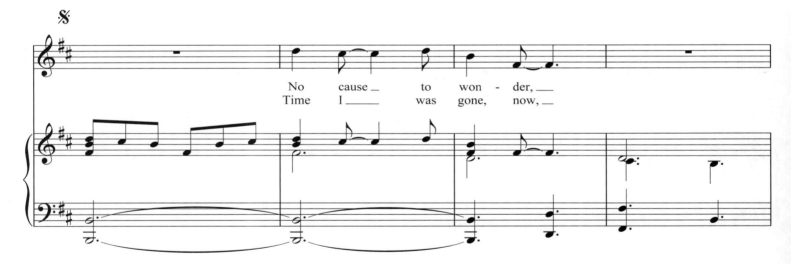

No cause to won - der, ___
Time I ___ was gone, now, ___

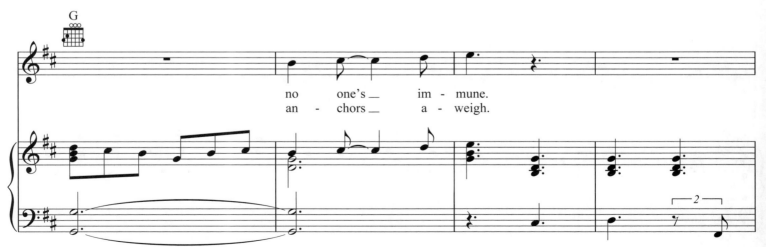

no one's ___ im - mune.
an - chors ___ a - weigh.

I kissed _ you un - der the
I'm mov - ing on, now, just

hunt - er's moon.
one more day.

You wan - der free, now. _
I'll let __ you go, now. _

Don't look for me, now.
How do we know, though,

To Coda ⊕

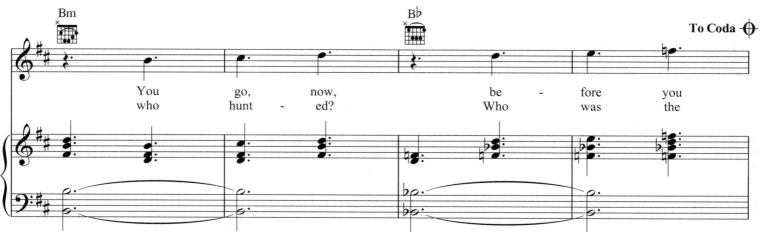

You go, now, be - fore you
who hunt - ed? Who - was you the

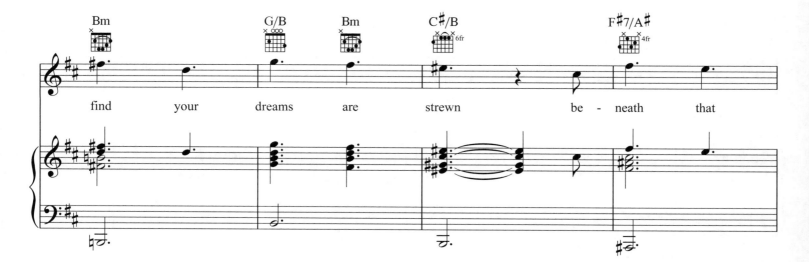

find your dreams are strewn be - neath that

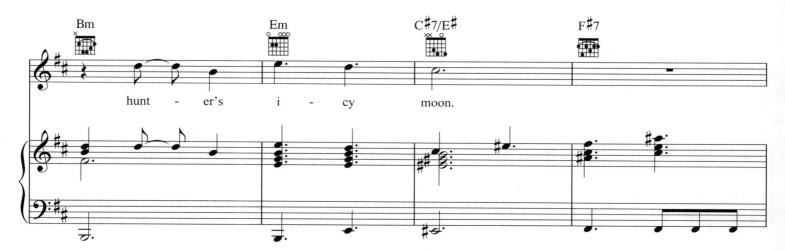

hunt - er's i - cy moon.

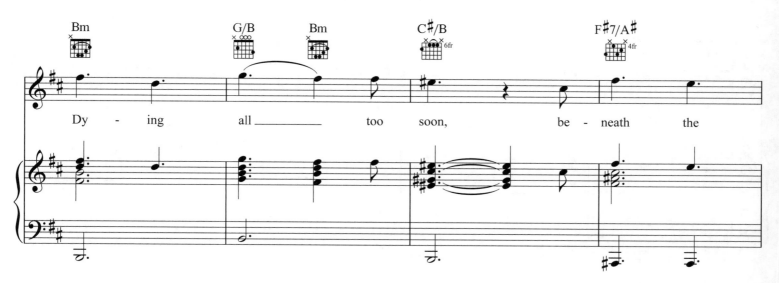

Dy - ing all _____ too soon, be - neath the

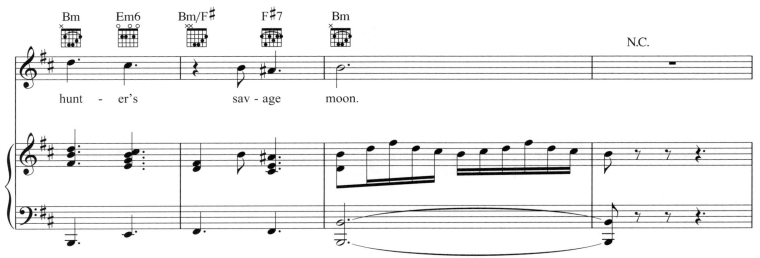

hunt - er's   sav - age   moon.

prey?

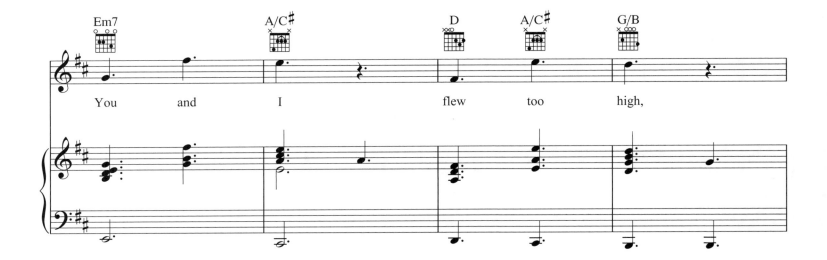

You   and   I   flew   too   high,

now we're __ fall - ing free,

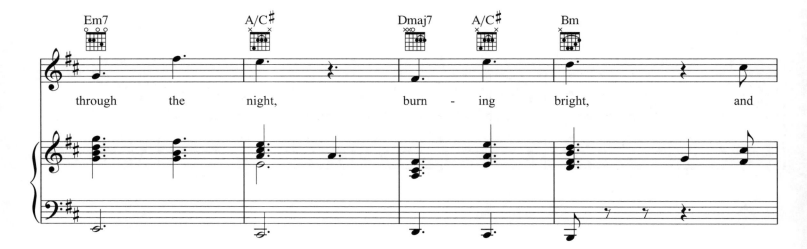

through the night, burn - ing bright, and

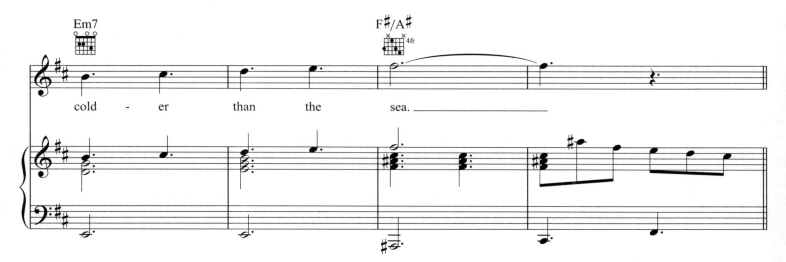

cold - er than the sea. _____

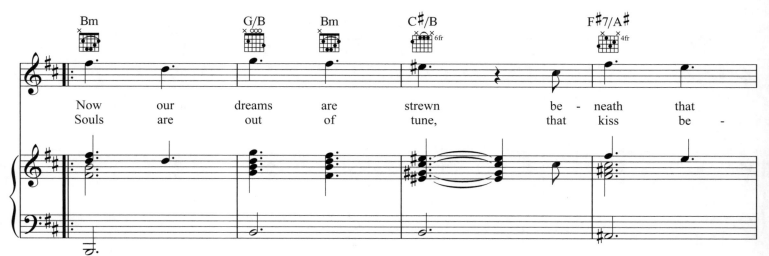

Now our dreams are strewn be - neath that
Souls are out of tune, that kiss be -

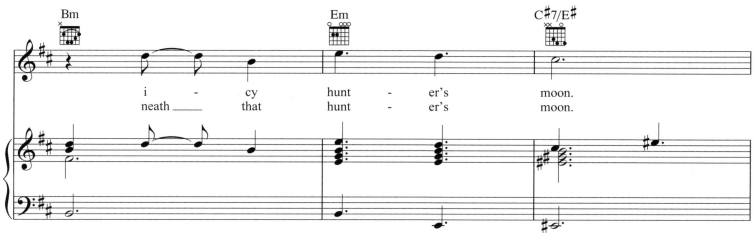

i - cy hunt - er's moon.
neath ____ that hunt - er's moon.

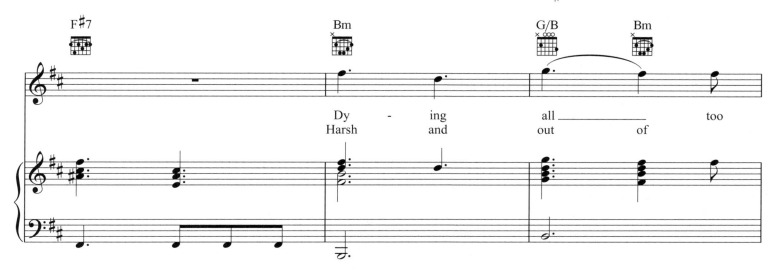

Dy - ing all _____ too
Harsh and out of

soon be - neath the hunt - er's
tune, and cursed the to

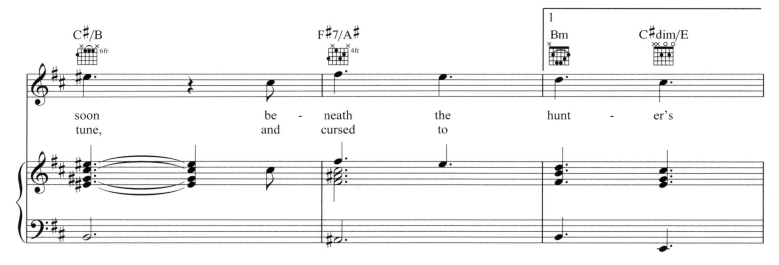

sav - age moon.

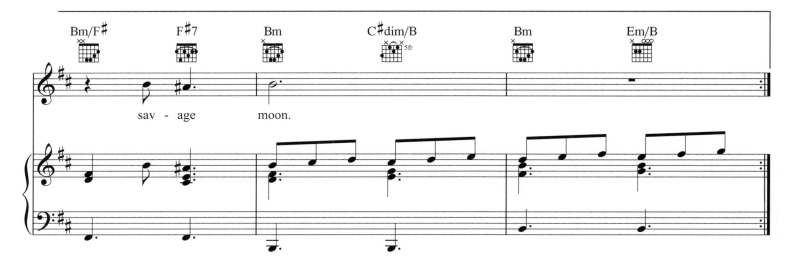

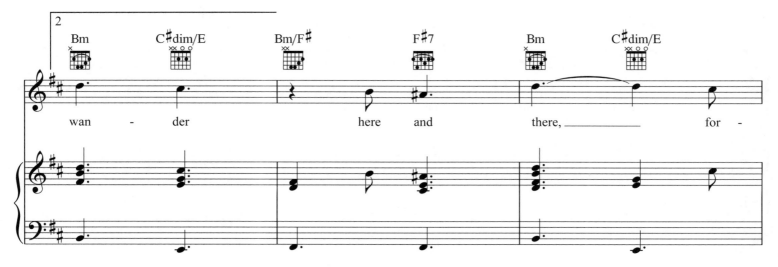

wan - der   here and   there, _____   for -

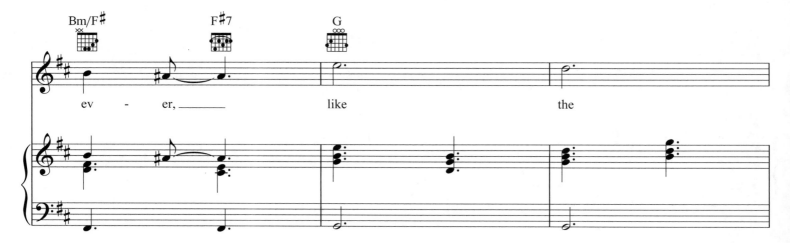

ev - er, _____   like   the

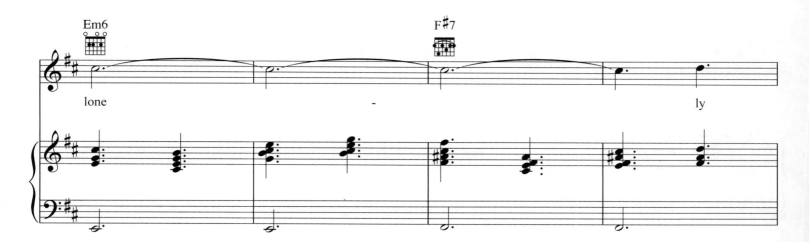

lone   -   ly

moon.

SHE MOVED THROUGH THE FAIR

Arranged by
DAVID MUNRO

72

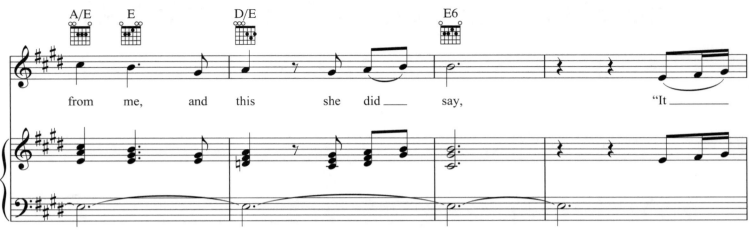

from me, and this she did ___ say, "It ___

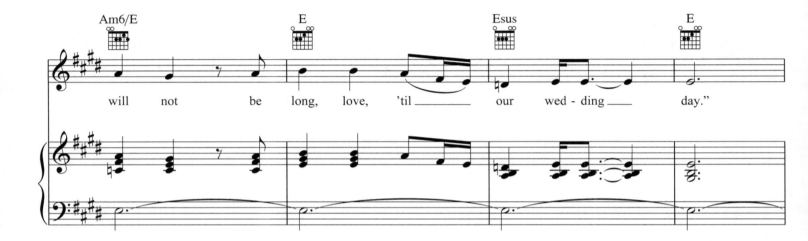

will not be long, love, 'til ___ our wed-ding ___ day."

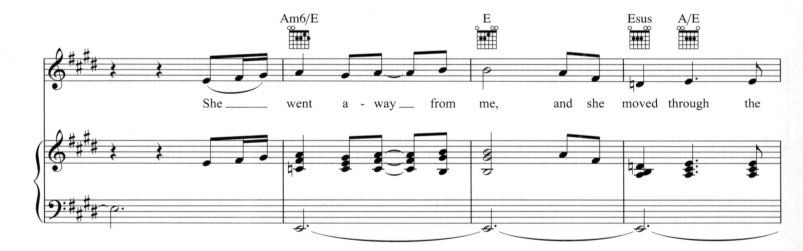

She ___ went a-way ___ from me, and she moved through the

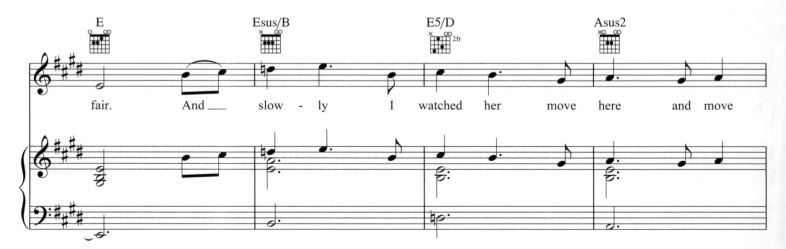

fair. And ___ slow-ly I watched her move here and move

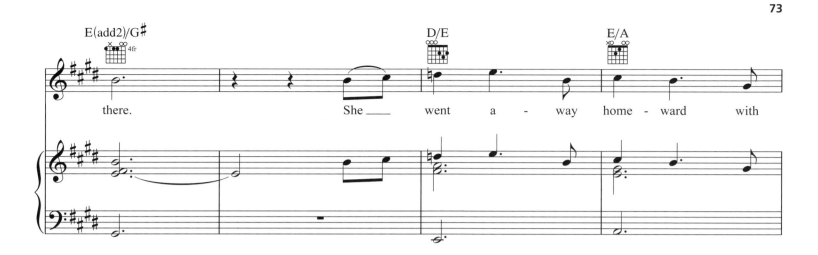

there. She ___ went a - way home - ward with

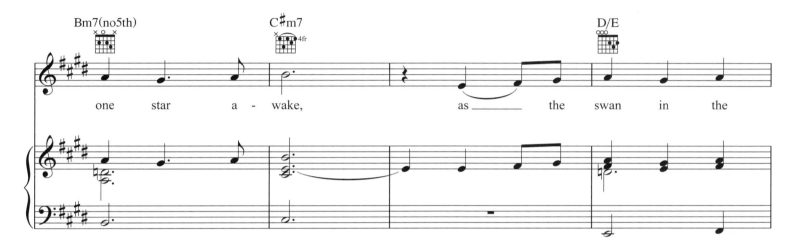

one star a - wake, as _____ the swan in the

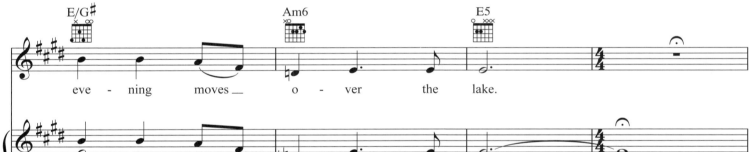

eve - ning moves ___ o - ver the lake.

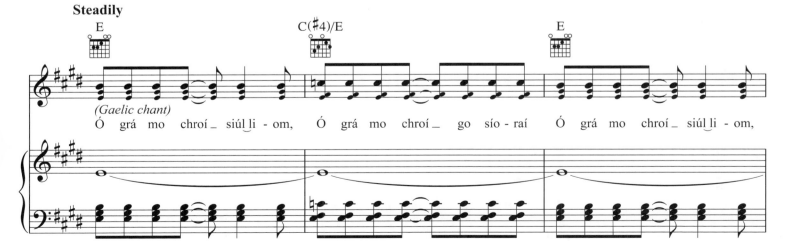

Steadily

(Gaelic chant)
Ó grá mo chroí ___ siúl li - om, Ó grá mo chroí ___ go sío - raí Ó grá mo chroí ___ siúl li - om,

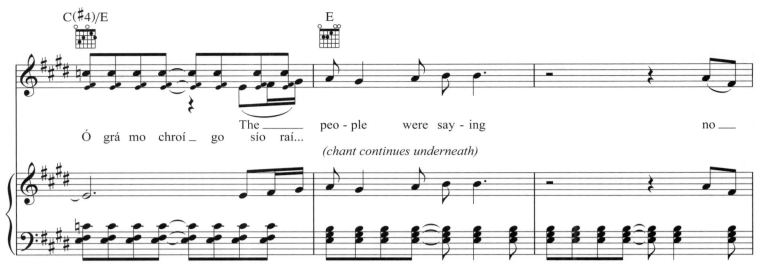

Ó grá mo chroí go sío raí...
The _____ peo - ple were say - ing no ___
(chant continues underneath)

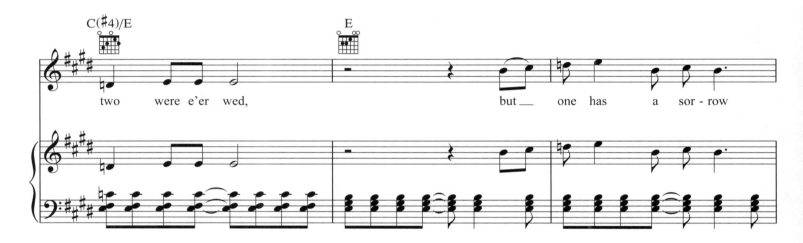

two were e'er wed, but ___ one has a sor - row

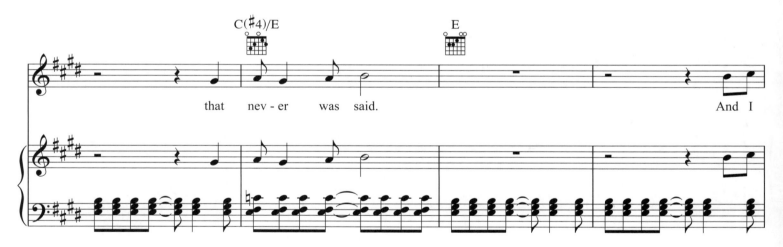

that nev - er was said. And I

smiled as she passed with her goods and her

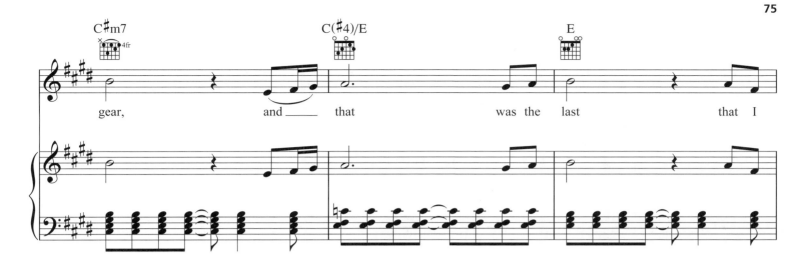

gear, and _____ that was the last that I

Freely, as before

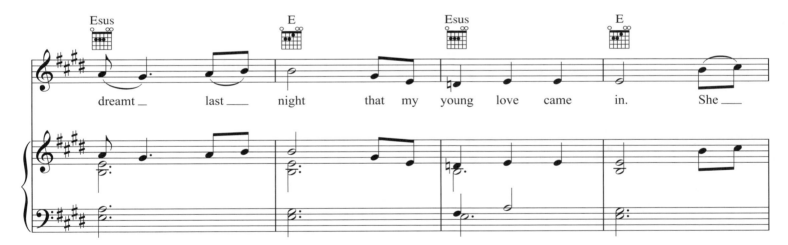

saw of my dear. I _____

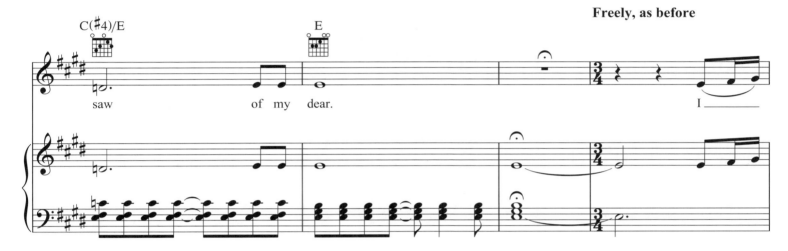

dreamt __ last ___ night that my young love came in. She ___

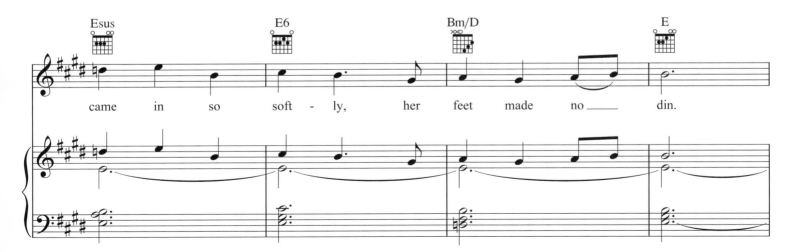

came in so soft - ly, her feet made no _____ din.

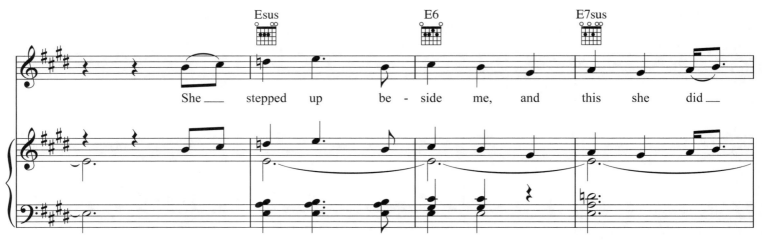

She __ stepped up be - side me, and this she did __

say, "It _____ will not be long, love, _____

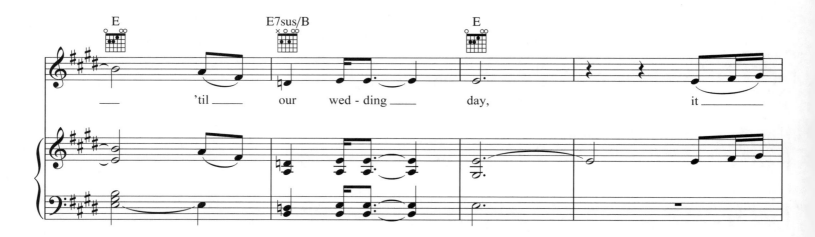

__ 'til ___ our wed - ding ___ day, it _____

will not be long, love, 'til _____ our wed - ding ___ day."

CAROLINA RUA

Words and Music by
THOM MOORE

Joyful Folk

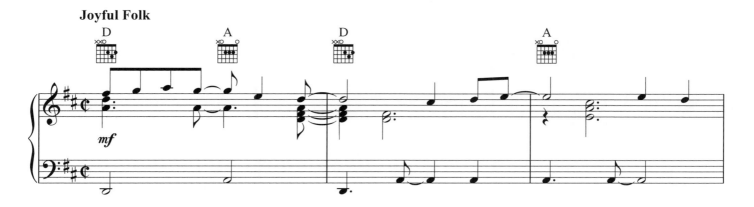

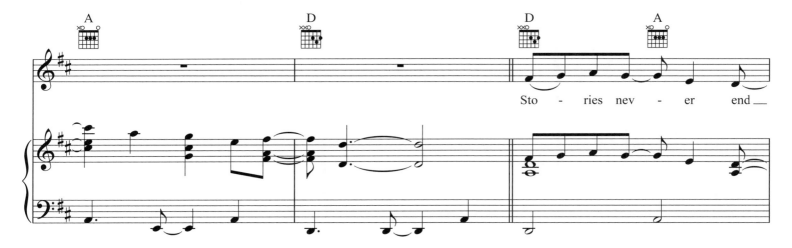

Sto - ries nev - er end __

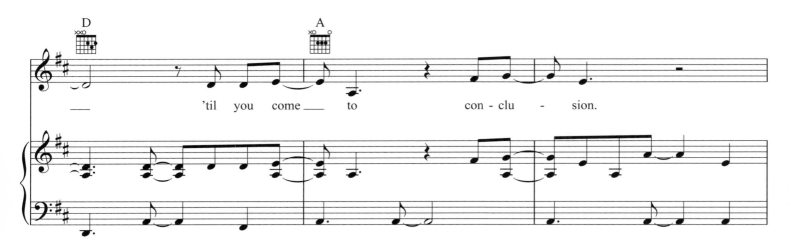

__ 'til you come __ to con - clu - sion.

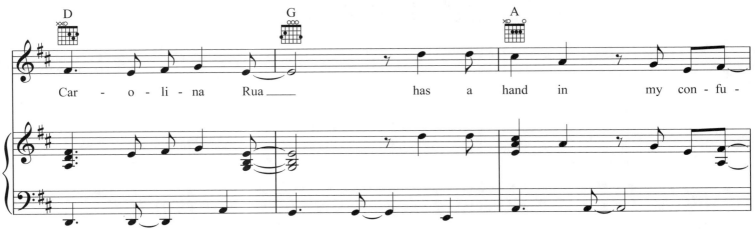

Car - o - li - na Rua___ has a hand in my con - fu -

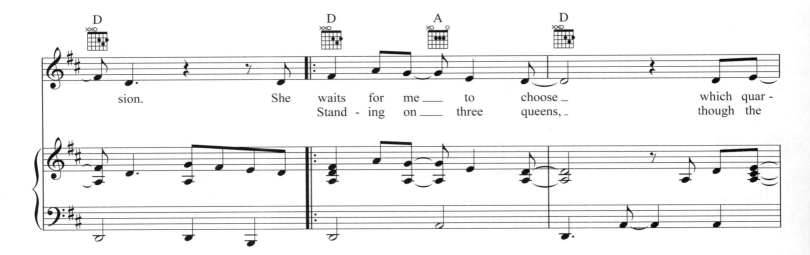

sion. She waits for me___ to choose___ which quar -
Stand - ing on___ three queens,_ though the

- ter to bend___ in, to Su - sie make me blue,_
game was o - ver. Then, out from the blue,_

___ or the red - head I'm at - tend - ing. Now
___ Car - o - li - na's at my shoul - der with

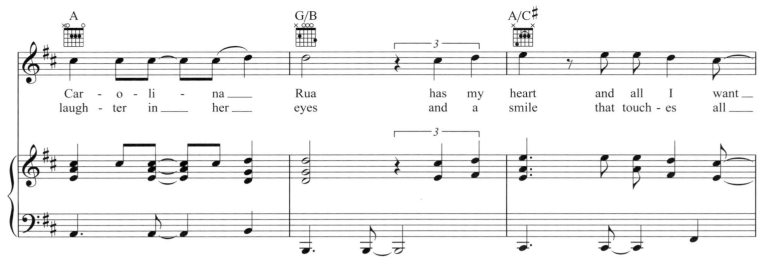

Car - o - li - na ___ Rua ___ has my heart ___ and all I want ___
laugh - ter in ___ her ___ eyes ___ and a smile ___ that touch - es all ___

___ to do ___ is go ___ down the wind - ing ___ road ___ where my
___ the guys. ___ on

Car - o - li - na goes, ___ down the crook - ed ___

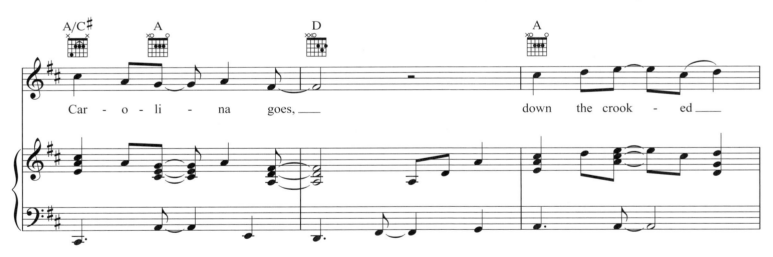

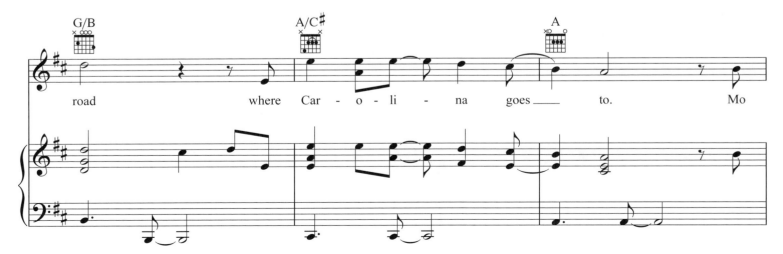

road ___ where Car - o - li - na goes ___ to. ___ Mo

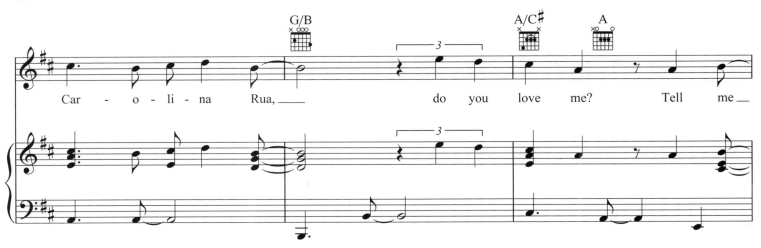

Car - o - li - na Rua, ____ do you love me? Tell me

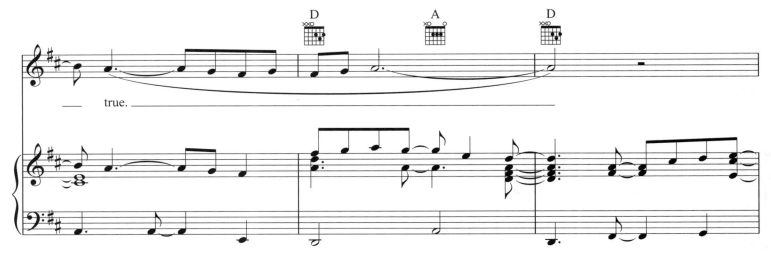

_ true. _____

Car - o - li - na, _____ oh. _

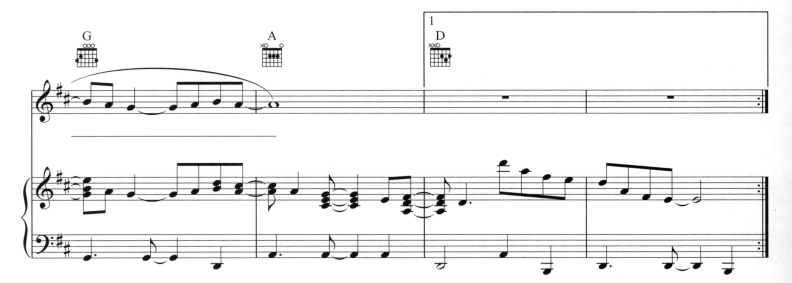

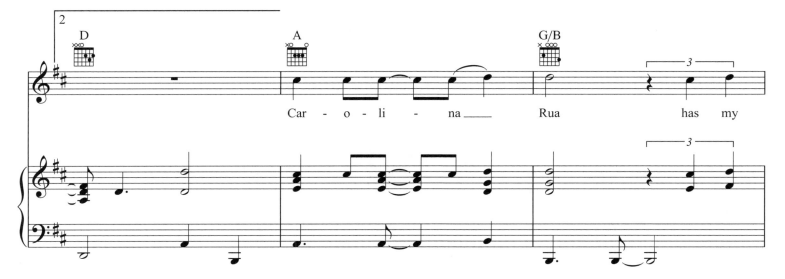

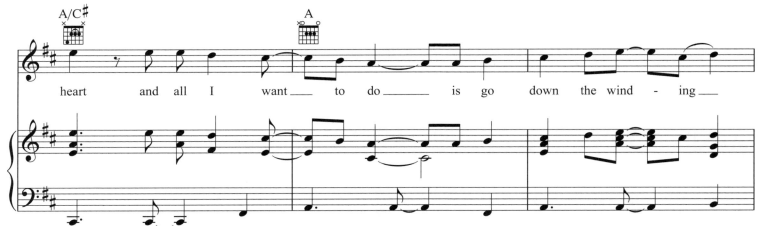

to. Mo Car - o - li - na Rua, _____ do you

love me? Tell me _____ true. _____

_____ Tell me _____ true. _____

Car - o - li - na Rua. _____

TURNING AWAY

Music and Lyrics by
DOUGIE MACLEAN

84

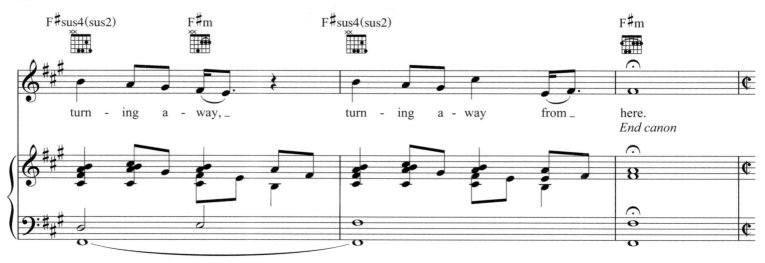

turn - ing a - way, _ turn - ing a - way from _ here.

End canon

Churning Anthem

On the wa - ter we ____ have walked like the
well up - on ____ the hill from our
Et - ive on they ____ have worked with their

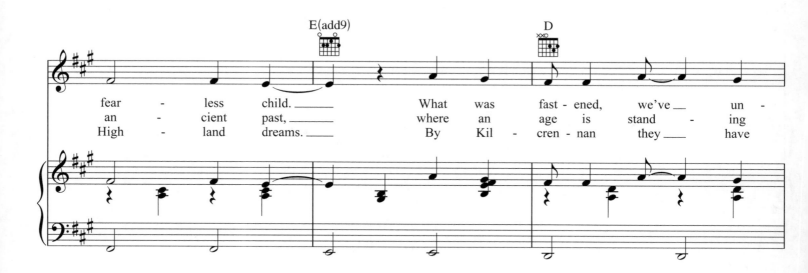

fear - less child. ____ What was fast - ened, we've ____ un -
an - cient past, ____ where an age is stand - ing
High - land dreams. ____ By Kil - cren - nan they ____ have

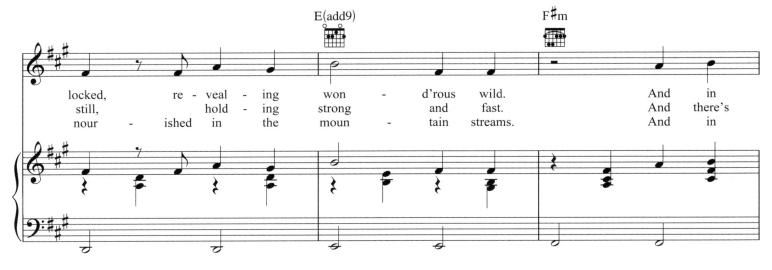

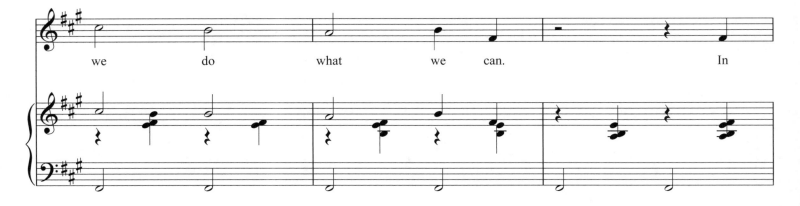

we   do   what   we   can.   In

day - light,   we're   ob - liv - i -

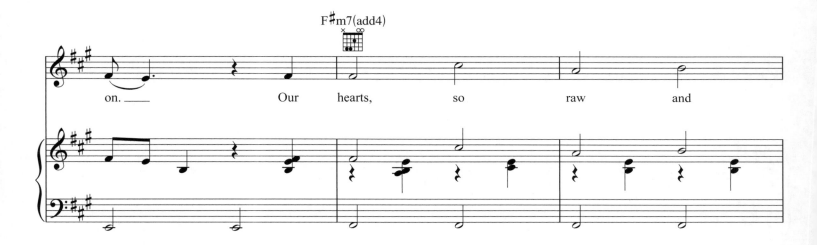

on. ____   Our   hearts,   so   raw   and

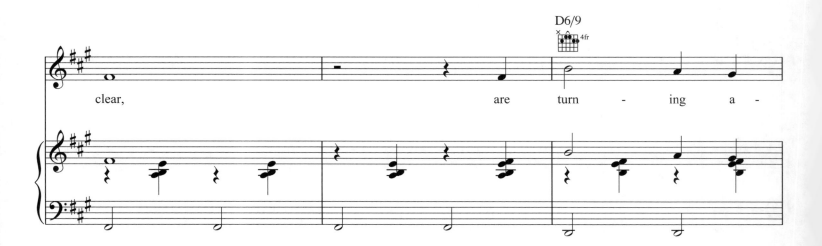

clear,   are   turn - ing   a -

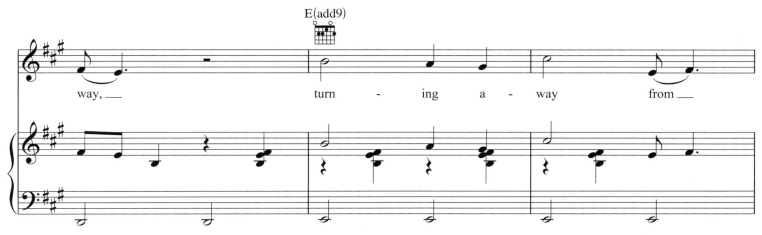

way, ___ turn - ing a - way from ___

here.

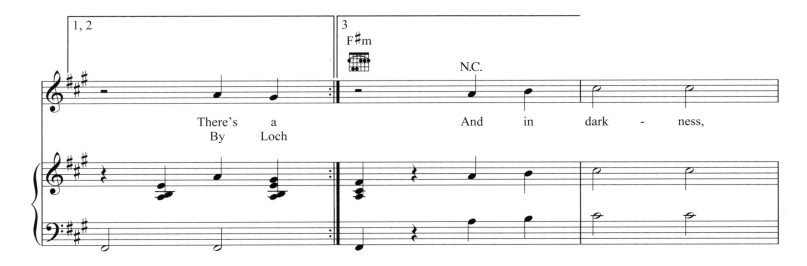

There's a
By Loch

And in dark - ness,

we do what we can. In

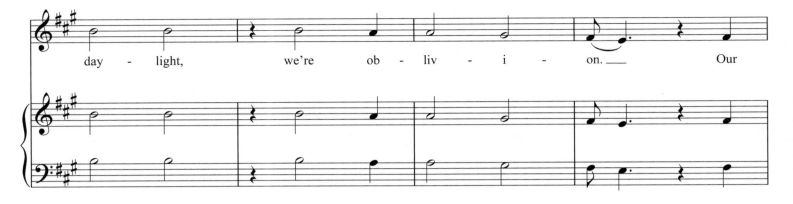

day - light, we're ob - liv - i - on. ___ Our

hearts, so raw and clear, are

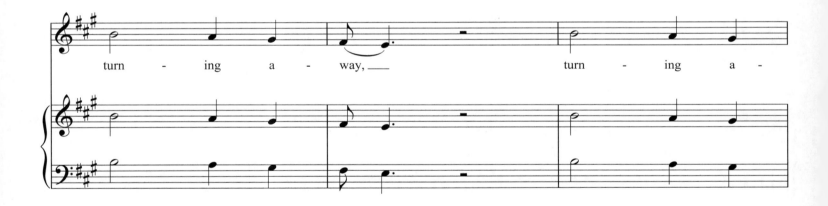

turn - ing a - way, ___ turn - ing a -

F#m7(add4)

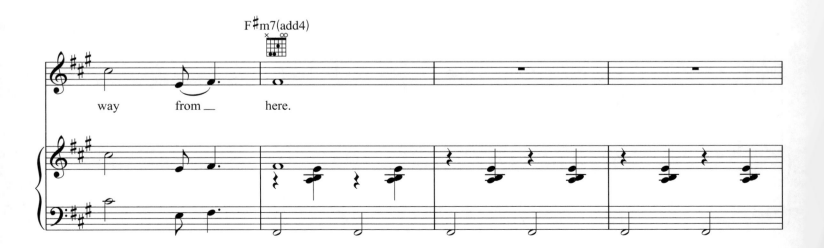

way from ___ here.

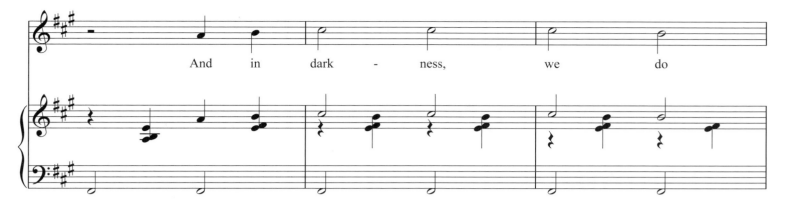

And in dark - ness, we do

what we can. In day - light,

D6/9

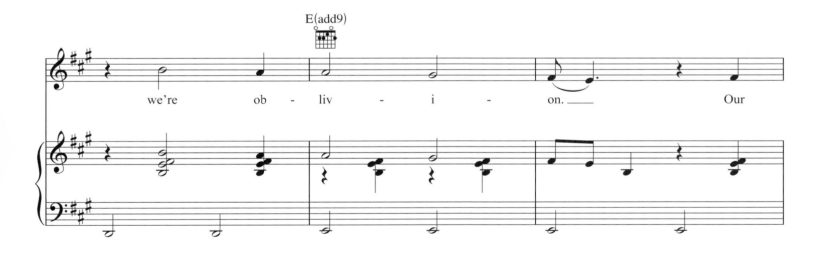

we're ob - liv - i - on. ___ Our

E(add9)

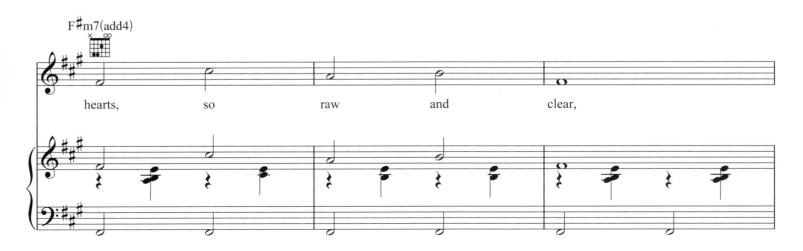

hearts, so raw and clear,

F#m7(add4)

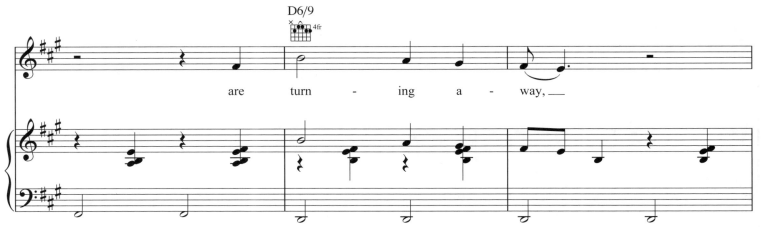

are turn - ing a - way, ____

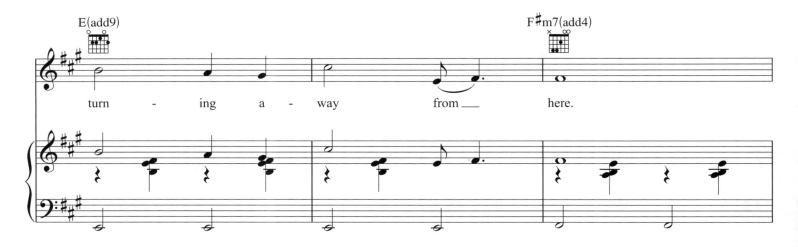

turn - ing a - way from ____ here.

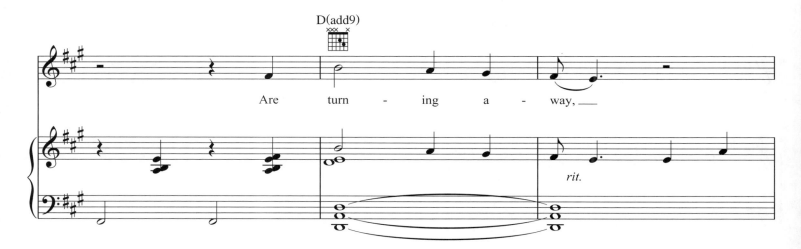

Are turn - ing a - way, ____

rit.

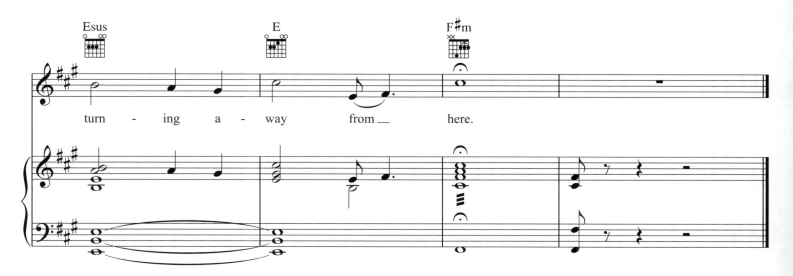

turn - ing a - way from ____ here.

TEARS OF HERCULES

Words and Music by MARC JORDAN
and STEPHAN MOCCIO

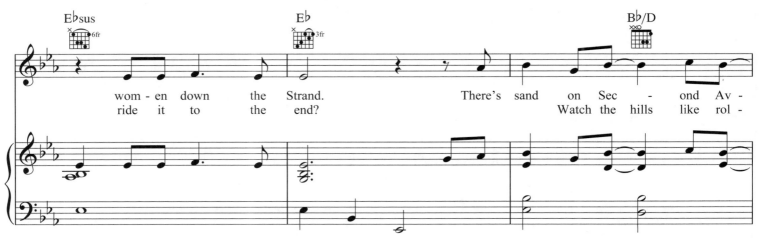

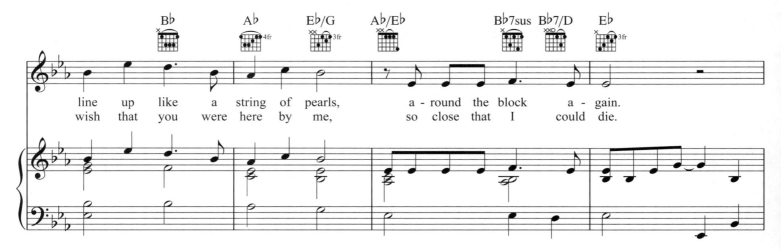

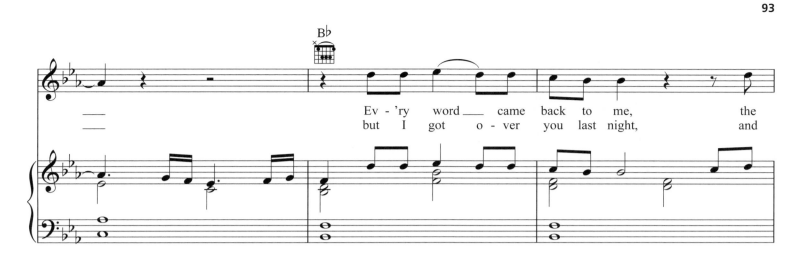

Ev - 'ry word ___ came back to me, ____ the
but I got o - ver you last night, ____ and

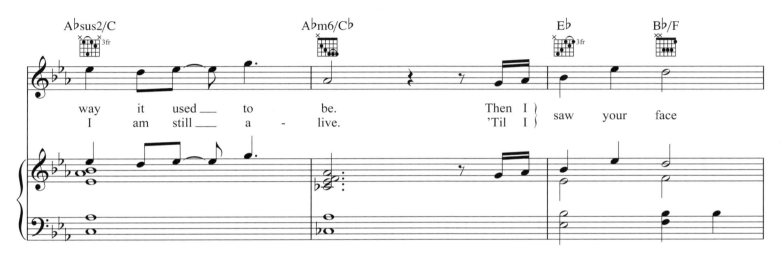

way it used ___ to be. ____ Then I
I am still ___ a - live. ____ 'Til I } saw your face

a-cross the street ____ through the tears ____ of Her - cu - les. _____

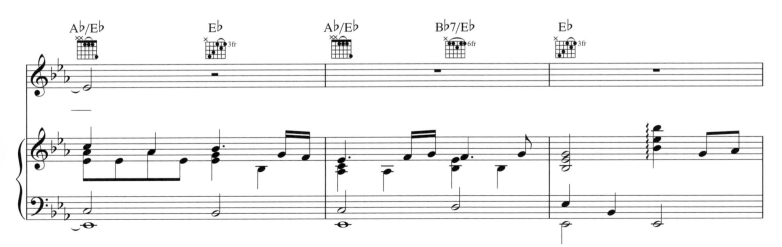

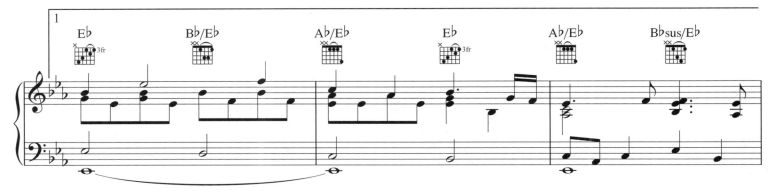

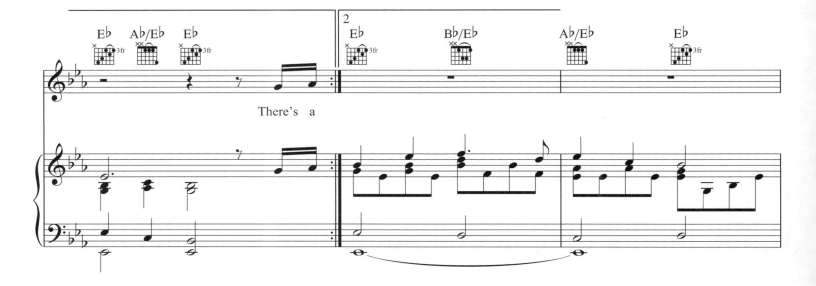

There's a

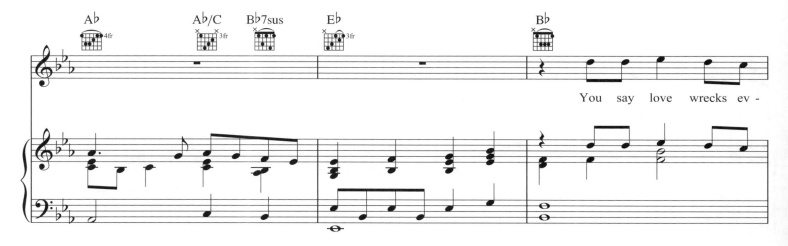

You say love wrecks ev -

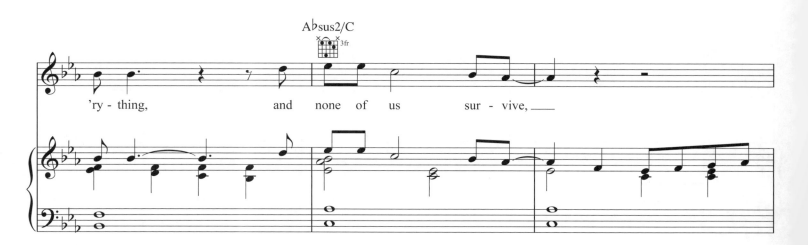

'ry - thing, and none of us sur - vive, ___

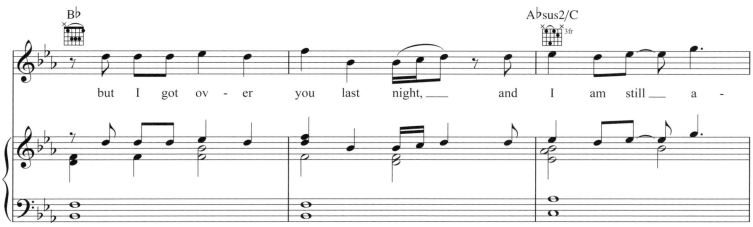

but I got ov - er you last night, ___ and I am still ___ a -

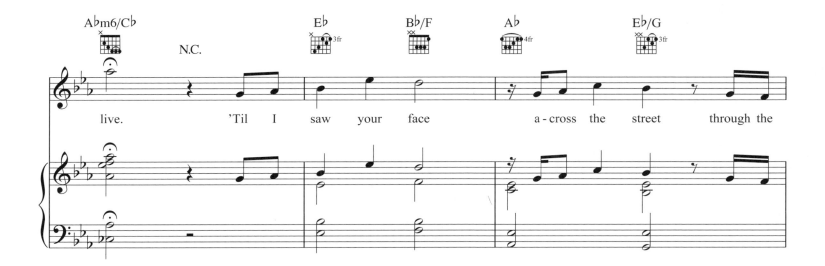

live. 'Til I saw your face a - cross the street through the

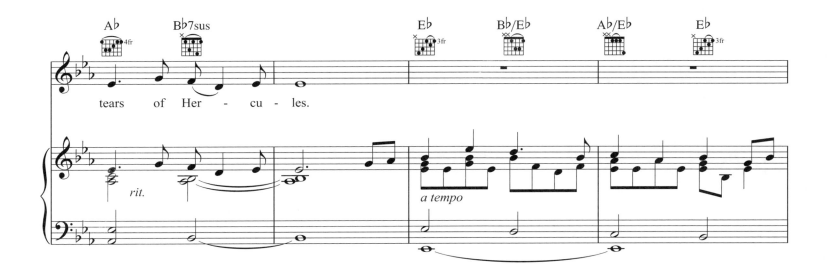

tears of Her - cu - les.

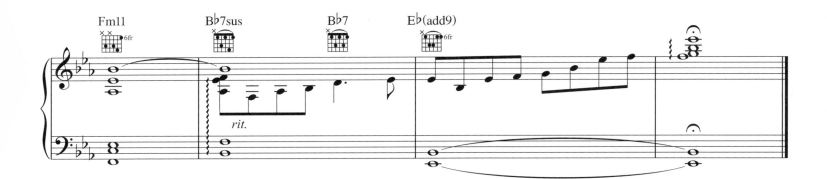

MY LAND

Words and Music by BRENDAN GRAHAM,
ALANA GRAHAM and ROLF LOVLAND

Pastoral, Hymn-like

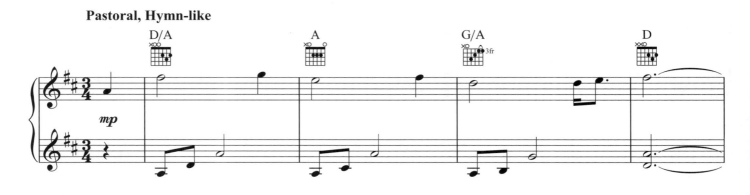

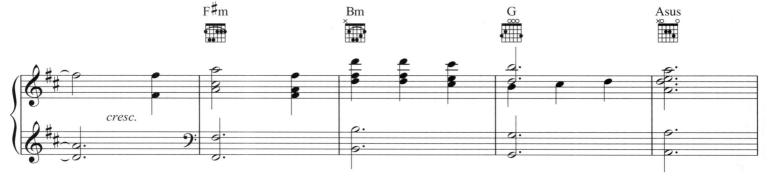

How

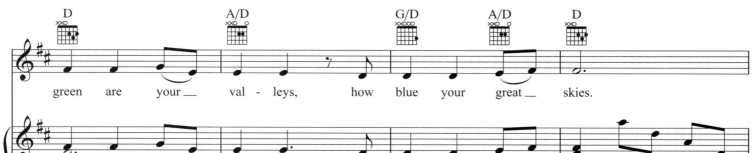

green are your __ val - leys, how blue your great __ skies.

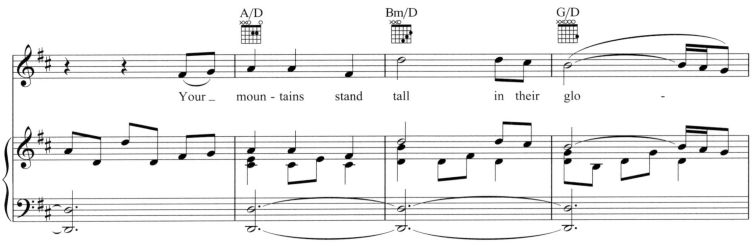

Your _ moun - tains stand tall in their glo -

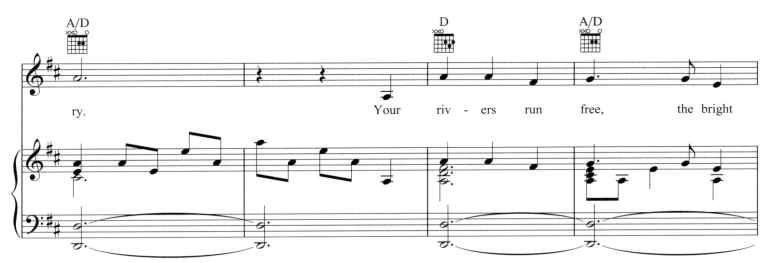

ry. Your riv - ers run free, the bright

stars are your eyes. Your beau - ty is

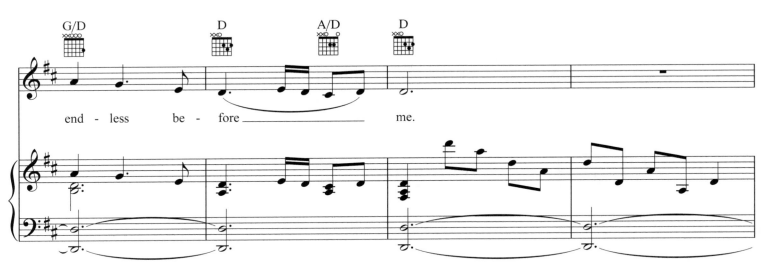

end - less be - fore _____ me.

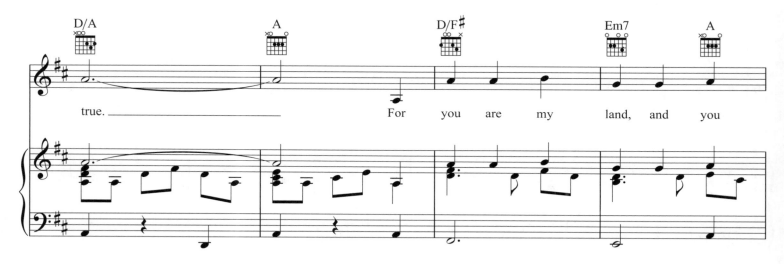

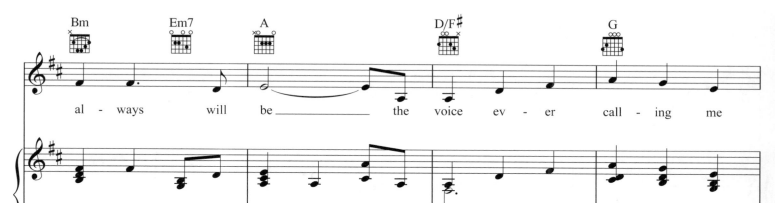

home   to   you.   When   times   we   are

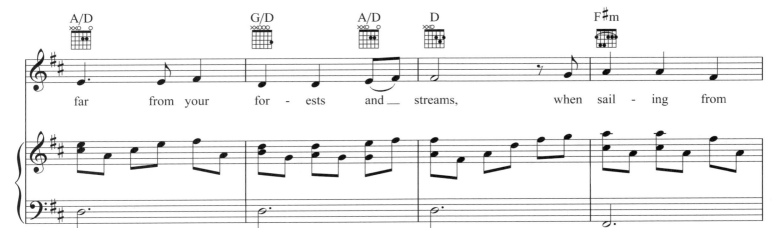

far   from your   for - ests   and __ streams,   when   sail - ing   from

your   shin - ing   wat -   ers,   we   car - ry   your

hopes,   your   spir - it,   your dreams,   in   the   hearts   of   your

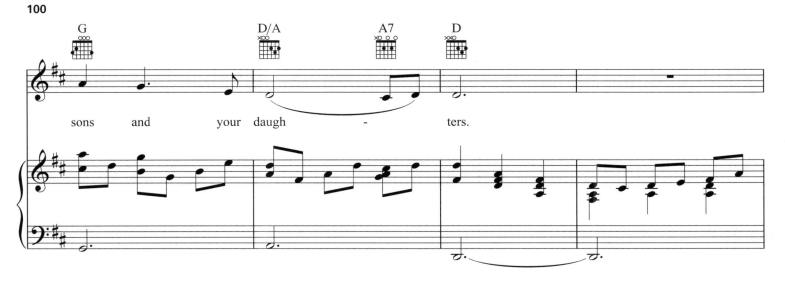

sons and your daugh - ters.

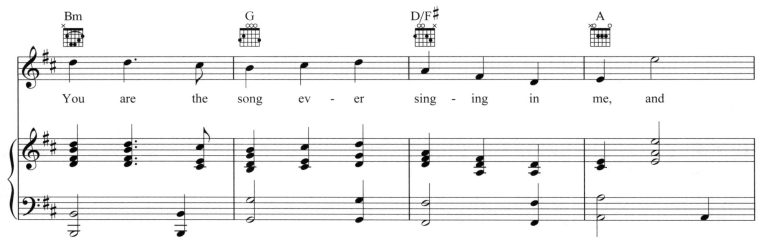

You are the song ev - er sing - ing in me, and

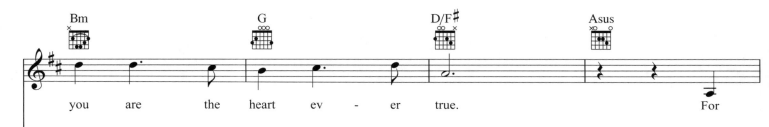

you are the heart ev - er true. For

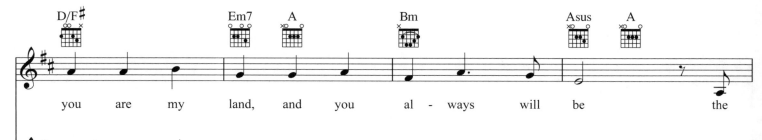

you are my land, and you al - ways will be the

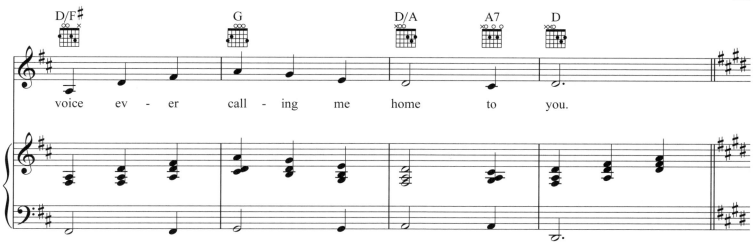

voice ev - er call - ing me home to you.

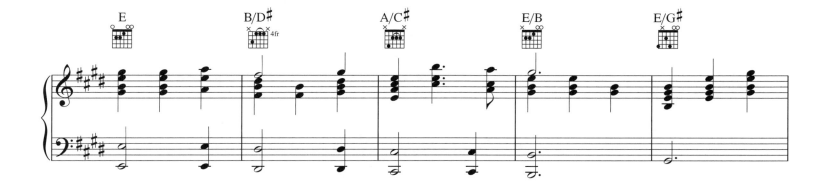

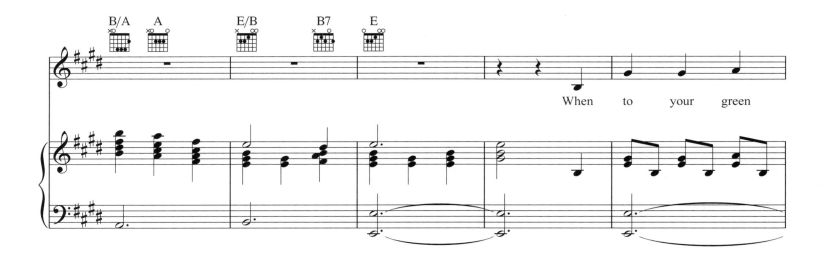

When to your green

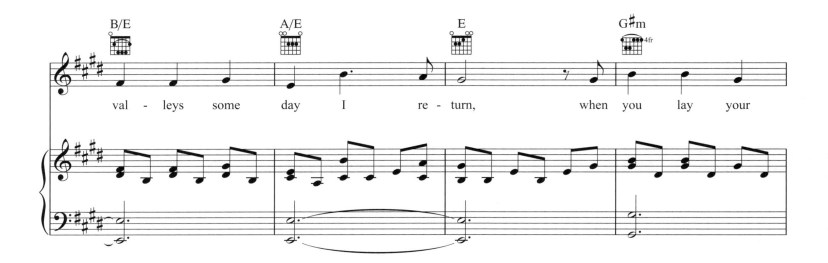

val - leys some day I re - turn, when you lay your

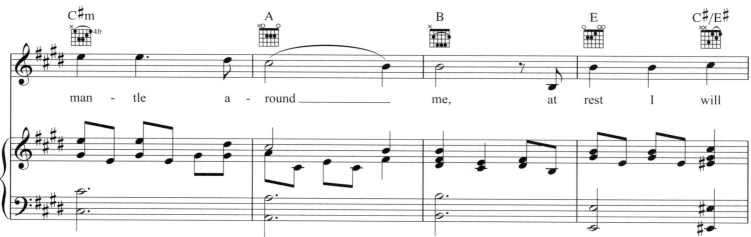

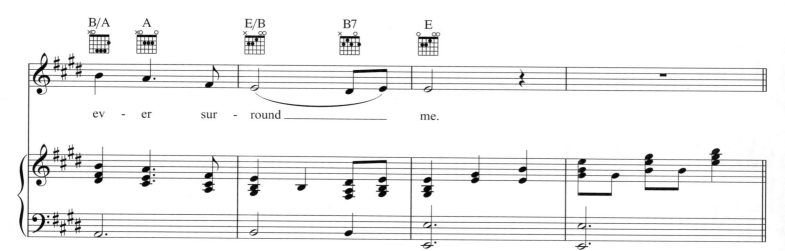

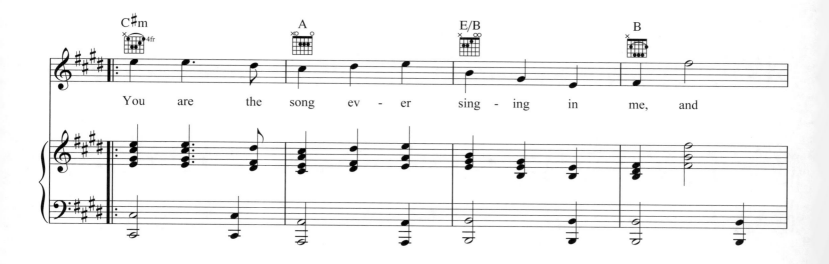

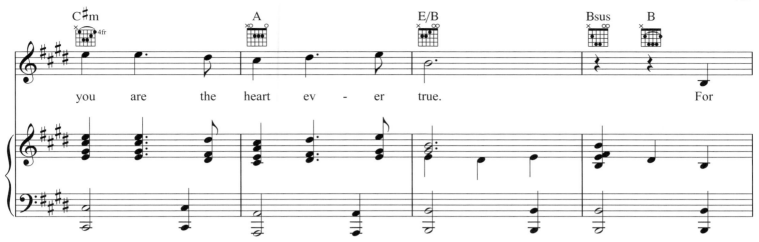

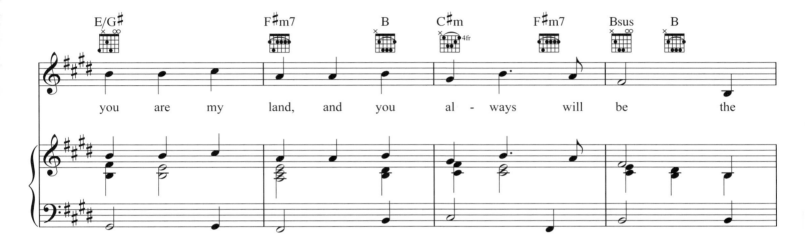

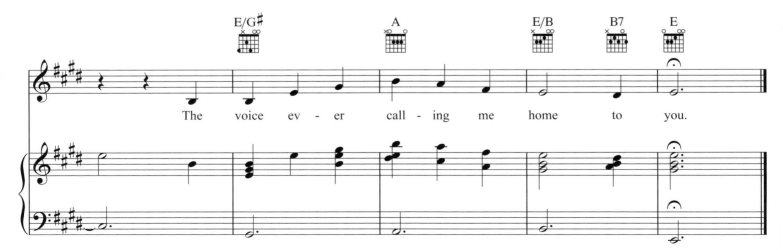